1999

ALCOHOL ABUSE

Straight Talk
Straight Answers

Pippa Sales

Ixia Publications
Honolulu, Hawaii

Publisher's Cataloging-in-Publication
(Provided by Quality Books, Inc.)

Sales, Pippa.
      Alcohol abuse : straight talk, straight answers /
Pippa Sales. -- 2nd ed.
      p. cm.
      Includes bibliographical references and index.
      LCCN: 98-73735
      ISBN: 1-884633-04-8

      1. Alcoholics--Family relationships
      2. Alcoholics--Rehabilitation. 3. Alcoholism
      I. Title

HV5132.S24 1999   362.29'2
                           QBI98-1614

For my family and friends
with love and thanks

They can because they think they can.

Virgil

WARNING AND DISCLAIMER

The author and publisher disclaim all liability in connection with the use and/or implementation of any information from this book.

The views expressed in this book are a summary of the current principles (research and evidence) on alcohol abuse and alcoholism as researched and expressed by experts in the field of alcohol abuse and alcoholism. Every effort has been made to make this book as complete and as accurate as possible.

The author and publisher are not responsible for any action taken as a result of reading this book. This book is intended as a general guide - an introduction to alcohol abuse and alcoholism and what can be done about it. This book is not a substitute for medical advice from a licensed physician or other professional trained in alcohol abuse and alcoholism.

A listing in the resource section does not represent an endorsement from the author or publisher. Neither do the author or publisher endorse any of the resource listings. The addresses and telephone numbers were current at the time of writing. The author and publisher regret any inconvenience due to subsequent changes.

TABLE OF CONTENTS

What is alcoholism? • What is alcohol abuse?
• What is an alcoholic? • Who becomes an
alcoholic? • What are the stages of alcoholism?
What causes alcoholism? • Why do alcoholics
take up drinking? • Why do alcoholics continue drinking and not seek help? • Do all
alcoholics drink a lot? • Is anyone who has a
problem with drinking or drinks a lot an alcoholic? • Is there a way to prevent becoming an
alcoholic?

How do I know if I or someone I care about is
dependent on alcohol? • Early warning signs. •
Telltale signs in the early, middle and late
stages. • Short self-test • A blackout is an
important telltale sign. What is a blackout and
how can I tell if someone is having a blackout?

What are the short-term effects of drinking?
What are the long-term effects of drinking?

What is a defense? • Why do alcoholics use
defenses? • What are some examples of defenses?

What is enabling? • What is an enabler? • Who can be an enabler? • What is some enabling behavior? • Why do people enable? • Why must I change my enabling behavior? • What can I do to change my enabling behavior? • What can happen if I change my enabling behavior?

What is an Intervention? • Why do an Intervention? • Who initiates an Intervention? • Do I have a right to Intervene? • Who is involved in an Intervention? • What steps do I take to prepare for an Intervention? • How long does an Intervention take? • Why does Intervention work? • What if the Intervention fails? • Can you do another Intervention if the initial Intervention does not achieve your goal? • Why don't more people do an Intervention?

What types of treatment are there available? • Do all alcohol abusers and alcoholics have to be treated as an inpatient? • Are all treatment centers the same? • What should you look for in a treatment center's program? • Who will pay for treatment? • Why is total abstinence so important? • Why is nutrition so important? • Do the family and I need to get treatment? • What is Alcoholics Anonymous and what are some of its principles? • What are some of the other support groups available and what are their principles? (Rational Recovery; Secular Organizations for Sobriety; and Women for Sobriety) • Is attending a support group important? • How important is the alcoholic's commitment to treatment and recovery? • Can a relapse happen if the alcoholic has had treatment? • Can drugs be used to treat alcoholics who repeatedly relapse? • Where do I find treatment centers, Alcoholics Anonymous and other support groups?

Is there any connection between smoking and drinking? • What is the relationship between alcohol and sleep? • Is there a problem with using alcohol as a tranquilizer to relieve stress? • Is there any relationship between suicide and drinking? • Does drinking make a person more aggressive or violent? • Is there a relationship between domestic violence and drinking? • What is the relationship between risky sexual behavior and drinking? • Are there any particular concerns for older people and drinking? • What are some facts about drinking and driving?

National Resources
State Authorities
Where to Find Help State by State

FOREWORD

When we ponder the various epidemics, diseases and plagues that have swept human populations throughout history, an eerie chill and a feeling of powerlessness overcome us. It is not surprising, therefore, that we take great pride and comfort in the accomplishment of modern scientific research and the hope it holds in finding cures and preventative measures for the diseases and the "curses" that visit mankind from time to time.

We look and listen for news of breakthroughs in search for cures to cancer, heart disease and AIDS. And, we examine, treat and inoculate our bodies in an effort to avoid such illnesses. Yet, at this very moment, one out of ten Americans is suffering from a widely ignored, progressive and potentially fatal disease. Very few of those afflicted are aware of their disease. Some of those afflicted will die and with their last breath deny the existence of this disease. This disease is alcoholism.

Alcoholism is not just a disease of the poor; it is not related to lack of proper sanitation or nutrition, although those living in poverty are also afflicted. Some studies suggest that the higher a person's education, the greater the person's income, the greater the incidence of the disease.

Surveys done by several Bar Associations indicate that from 15 to 20 percent of lawyers are or will become alcoholics. That fact has always puzzled me. In my work counseling attorneys and judges I have learned of their interest in maintaining good health. They show concern about their weight, their cholesterol levels and blood pressure. They have access to the finest medical care available. So how is it they do not take action against this life-destroying disease?

There are two main reasons. The first is the lack of education of the symptoms, the progression, the nature of the disease itself and the treatment available. The second reason is inherent in the nature of the disease. Alcoholism is not only a devastating disease. Alcoholism carries with its destructiveness a very effective mechanism which hides the disease from the awareness of the victim. This defense is called denial.

Denial makes it almost impossible for the alcoholic to realize the mental, physical, emotional and spiritual debilitation he or she may be enduring. The alcoholic is usually the last person in the world to acknowledge the extent of his or her addiction.

If we, as a caring society, wish to arrest this epidemic we must educate not only alcoholics but those around the alcoholics who can lead them out of the darkness of denial.

It is for this purpose that Pippa Sales has written *Alcohol Abuse: Straight Talk, Straight Answers*. Pippa addresses the significant issues pertaining to alcoholism and recovery in a clear and concise manner. Her book is a great help to many people in the community who are suffering from alcoholism, or have friends or relatives suffering. The brief and clear language in this book makes sense to all affected by alcoholism, even those who are so emotionally entangled with the disease that they thought help was beyond hope.

Pippa's efforts are of great benefit to society.

Peter Donahoe, J.D., Director
Attorneys and Judges Assistance Program
Supreme Court, State of Hawaii

CHAPTER 1

The Cost of Alcohol Abuse and Alcoholism to the Nation

"Alcohol can kill."

Alcoholism is not just a disease. Alcohol abuse is the number one health problem in the United States. Alcohol abuse and alcoholism together are the number three killer in the United States after cancer and heart disease. There are over 18 million alcohol abusers and alcoholics in the United States.

Alcohol is a factor in over half of all manslaughters, assaults, rapes, spousal abuse, murders, attempted murders, robberies, and burglaries. Alcohol is frequently a factor in motor vehicle accidents, suicides, fires, burns and drownings. Alcohol kills more people each year than all illegal drugs combined and is the most commonly abused drug in our society.

In the workplace, employees who abuse alcohol are less productive and are more likely to cause workplace injuries to themselves and others. In addition, employees who abuse alcohol are late for work five times more frequently, use three times more sick leave and are absent from the job sixteen times more often than employees who do not abuse alcohol. Even a nonalcoholic employee who is a member of an alcoholic family uses an average of ten times more sick leave than normal.

In short, people die from alcohol abuse and alcoholism and the cost to the nation is staggering.

For each person who has the disease of alcoholism, at least four other people are directly affected by that person's alcoholism. That is a lot of people suffering in this country. The tragedy is that few people do anything about their own or another person's alcoholism. Or, they wait until the disease is so advanced that the person suffering from alcoholism is severely physically and mentally harmed.

You **can** do something about alcoholism. The sooner you help an alcoholic to treatment the greater the chance of recovery. Alcoholism is the most untreated treatable disease in the United States. Often the people closest to the alcoholic find it hardest to see and admit that someone they care about is an alcoholic. These people, however, are the very ones who can help break the vicious cycle of the disease and are in the position to intervene. How long do you want to watch the self destruction of someone you care about?

In spite of all the trouble that drinking may cause, few people want to admit that they or someone they care about has a drinking problem or may be an alcoholic. Historically, there has been a stigma attached to the word alcoholic. No more. There is no need to feel ashamed. Alcoholism is a disease like any other disease and needs to be treated. It is a disease just as cancer, diabetes or heart disease are diseases. If someone you care about had one of these diseases you would get help for that person, wouldn't you?

The answer is to guide the person you care about to help for his or her alcoholism. The deceptive nature of the disease makes it hard for alcoholics to recognize their problem or to do anything about it. The disease allows alcoholics to live in a state of denial. If you accept this denial, the alcoholic could die. The alcoholic needs a helping hand to get to treatment and onto the road of recovery.

This book is for those of you who abuse alcohol or are an alcoholic and for those of you who care about someone who abuses alcohol or is an alcoholic. The goal of this book is to offer you a better understanding of:

- alcohol abuse and alcoholism;
- why alcoholics have difficulty in seeking the help they desperately need;
- how the abuse of alcohol affects the alcohol abuser or alcoholic and those closest to them;
- how you can do something to guide the alcohol abuser or alcoholic to treatment by Intervention; and,
- where you can find help in the area where you live.

If each of us helped guide one alcoholic to treatment, we would not only be helping that one person but the whole nation. With fewer alcoholics drinking, we would live in a healthier and safer country. We would have fewer motor vehicle accidents, less crime, less spouse and child abuse, less property destruction, less fire destruction, and fewer people in jails.

We can measure the financial cost to society of alcohol abuse and alcoholism but we cannot measure the pain, suffering, and family disruptions that it causes. Why suffer any more? Get help - for you and the alcohol abuser or alcoholic.

This book is the first of many steps, a guide to get you to **do** something to help yourself or someone you care about; to do something before a disaster strikes. You do not want anyone you know to become a statistic. There is so much help available that there is no reason why you cannot get help **now**!

Bacchus has drowned more men than Neptune.

Guiseppe Garibaldi

CHAPTER 2

Alcohol Abuse and the Disease of Alcoholism

"Nobody wants to become an alcoholic."

The issue of how to define alcohol abuse and alcoholism or alcohol dependency has been the subject of scholarly debate. There has been considerable disagreement in the alcohol field about what constitutes an alcohol problem, who has a problem, how to diagnose the problem, and how to describe or categorize the diagnosis once it has been made - is the person a problem drinker, alcohol abuser, harmful user, alcoholic or alcohol dependent? There is an obvious need for standardized criteria to diagnose alcohol problems and standardized terminology to describe a diagnosis. Standardization allows for everyone in the alcohol field to "speak the same language," diagnose alcohol problems according to set criteria, use the accepted definition and terminology for alcohol problems and provide the appropriate and best treatment for a person with a drinking problem.

Currently, the accepted terms for someone with a drinking problem are alcohol abuser and alcoholic or alcohol dependent. Both abuse alcohol and experience many of the same harmful effects of drinking. The main difference between the terms is that the alcohol abuser is not dependent on alcohol - does not have a physical dependence - whereas, an alcoholic or alcohol dependent person is physically dependent on alcohol, suffers from the disease of alcoholism or alcohol dependency, and has an impaired ability to control his or her alcohol intake.

The terms alcoholic or alcohol dependent, and alcoholism or alcohol dependency are one and the same. For clarity, this book uses the terms alcoholic and alcoholism, and alcohol abuser. Whatever terminology is used, however, both the alcohol abuser and alcoholic have a problem with drinking, abuse alcohol, and need help.

What is alcoholism?

Alcoholism is a powerful, life-threatening disease.

A person with alcoholism is physically dependent on alcohol and has a strong compulsion to drink. The nature of the disease affects the body and brain in such a way that the person has no control over his or her drinking. In fact, the drinking controls the alcoholic.

Alcoholism is a primary, chronic, progressive and potentially fatal disease. It is both diagnosable and treatable - it cannot be cured but it can be treated and arrested.

By primary it is meant that alcoholism is a disease itself and not caused by a social, emotional, or physical problem. In fact, it is the dependency on alcohol that causes many of the alcoholic's problems and these cannot be treated effectively unless the drinking stops.

By chronic it is meant that the disease is long lasting and there is no known cure for it. Alcoholism can be controlled - but not cured - by not drinking. It is regarded as the most untreated treatable disease in the United States.

By progressive it is meant that the disease will only worsen over time as long as alcohol is consumed and the alcoholism is left untreated. Alcoholism tends to progress through set stages - early, middle, late - with some alcoholics showing more extreme symptoms than others.

By fatal it is meant that if the alcoholism is left unchecked and the alcoholic does not stop drinking, the alcoholic will likely die from the disease.

Alcoholism is a serious disease that needs to, and can be treated. Understanding that alcoholism is a disease helps us to get help for the alcoholic and to treat him or her as we would a cancer, diabetes or heart disease sufferer. Since alcoholism, like diabetes, is treatable but not curable, recovery from alcoholism lasts a lifetime.

What is alcohol abuse?

Alcohol abuse refers to patterns of problem drinking that result in health consequences and social problems but falls short of alcoholism - the person does not have a susceptibility for alcoholism and is not physically dependent on alcohol. While alcohol abuse is essentially different from alcoholism, the line between them is difficult to draw because many of the effects of alcoholism are also experienced by alcohol abusers.

Alcohol abuse is still a harmful use of alcohol with as many as 40 million people in the United States abusing alcohol regularly or occasionally. Alcohol abusers are in need of help as much as alcoholics. You do not need to be an alcoholic to experience problems from alcohol. Any abuse of alcohol can have negative consequences that come from drinking too much such as problems at home, school or work; legal difficulties; a DUI (driving under the influence) conviction; or health problems.

Alcohol abusers are also termed problem drinkers but in reality both alcoholics and alcohol abusers are problem drinkers, the main difference being that the alcoholic is dependent on alcohol whereas the alcohol abuser is not. Alcohol abusers also tend to have a shorter history of problem drinking, usually from five to ten years and do not have a history of severe alcohol withdrawals. An alcohol abuser, unlike an alcoholic, can become a social user of alcohol or abstain later in life.

What is an alcoholic?

An alcoholic is a person who suffers from the disease of alcoholism.

Alcoholics are people who are dependent on alcohol because their bodies are incapable of processing alcohol normally. Something has gone very wrong inside their bodies and the only way the disease can be halted is by not drinking.

Who becomes an alcoholic?

The disease of alcoholism can affect anyone - it does not care how old you are, what sex you are, what color you are, what religion you belong to, or how much money you make. Most alcoholics do not conform to the "Skid Row" stereotype but are regular people with jobs, families and the usual responsibilities that go with life. To become an alcoholic you do need to have a susceptibility for the disease and you have to drink. A person who does not drink cannot become an alcoholic.

Most people who drink do not become alcoholics. If a person is not susceptible to alcoholism he or she will not become an alcoholic. Although not alcoholic, some of these people may have a problem with abusing alcohol, show many of the same symptoms as the alcoholic and, as a result, need help.

What are the stages of alcoholism?

1. Early or adaptive stage: The alcoholic may appear only as a heavy drinker. Drinking may be daily or less frequent and may be heavy only occasionally. The cells in the alcoholic's body are adapting to alcohol and allowing alcohol into the body in increasing amounts. Nonalcoholic alcohol abusers will show

many of the symptoms associated with the early stages of the disease.

2. Middle or dependent stage: The cells in the alcoholic's body become dependent on alcohol. There are many alterations in the normal functioning of cells of the body and the disease can no longer remain hidden. The alcoholic is now dependent on alcohol - the need for alcohol can feel as strong as the need for food or water.

3. Late or deteriorative stage: Alcohol seriously affects the alcoholic's mental, emotional and physical health. There is damage to vital organs in the body and the alcoholic has a lowered resistance to infection and other diseases. At this stage the alcoholic cannot understand that alcohol is destroying him or her.

4. Final stage: Death

What causes alcoholism?

Current evidence suggests that alcoholism is a result of genetic and environmental factors, and possibly psychological factors.

Environmental factors include cultural influences, social influences of family and friends, easy access to alcohol, stress and a host of influences that shape our thinking about alcohol and affects our drinking behavior.

It appears that genes and the environment interact to influence susceptibility to alcoholism and that both contribute to the development of alcoholism. Research into whether genetic influences or environmental influences are more important is not conclusive and is ongoing. Research into understanding which genes are responsible for a person's susceptibility to alcoholism is also ongoing.

Current research is exploring the role that psychological factors may play in the cause of alcoholism and how these factors interplay with the genetic and environmental factors.

The results of the current research answer some basic questions about alcoholism and how it can be prevented and treated. For example, knowing that alcoholism runs in families makes it easier to identify those at greatest risk of becoming an alcoholic so that they can take appropriate preventative steps.

Why do alcoholics take up drinking?

In our society, alcohol is available everywhere and a person really has to make a choice **not** to drink. Alcoholics start drinking for the same reasons that other people do. Alcohol can make people feel euphoric, stimulated, relaxed, or slightly intoxicated and is used with meals, in celebratory situations, in religious ceremonies or to enhance a social occasion. If asked why they drink, most people will answer with one of the following - to relax, to socialize, to celebrate, to go to sleep, to fit in with peers, to feel romantic, to make a business associate feel comfortable, to relieve stress, to forget problems, to relieve an ache or pain, or to get drunk.

Initially, in small amounts, alcohol is a stimulant and it is this effect that attracts people to drink. In large amounts - this amount varying from person to person - alcohol is a sedative. The difference between alcoholics and other drinkers is that the alcoholic will continue to drink even after the desired stimulating physical effects have been felt.

Why do alcoholics continue drinking and not seek help?

They cannot help it. The nature of the disease prevents alcoholics from realizing that they are dependent on alcohol. The alcohol alters alcoholics' thinking and reasoning "tricking" alcoholics into believing they can handle their drinking. Once the alcohol has chemically and electrically disturbed alcoholics' brains, they do not see their behavior the way others do. They do not see or accept what is happening to them. The alcoholic is physically dependent.

It is important to remember that a person is probably an alcoholic by the time he or she begins to act like an alcoholic. By the time it is evident that a person may be an alcoholic, the nature of the disease prevents him or her from having control over drinking. The drinking now controls the alcoholic and he or she continues to drink.

Do all alcoholics drink a lot?

No. You do not have to drink a lot or over an extended period of time to develop alcoholism. The effect alcohol has on a person is a very individual reaction. Alcoholics are characterized by how they drink - for example, in an uncontrolled way - not by how much or how often.

Is anyone who has a problem with drinking or drinks a lot an alcoholic?

> No. Alcohol is a selectively addictive drug. Not all people who drink heavily become alcoholics. The nonalcoholic alcohol abuser, however, has a drinking problem and needs help as much as the alcoholic to alleviate the psychological, physical and social problems caused by drinking too much.

Is there a way to prevent becoming an alcoholic?

> Do not drink! Without alcohol, there can be no alcoholism.

The man takes a drink; the drink takes a drink; and then the drink takes the man.

Chinese saying

CHAPTER 3

Telltale Signs of Alcoholism

"There is no alcoholic personality."

How do I know if I or someone I care about is dependent on alcohol?

If you question whether you or someone you care about has a problem with alcohol, you, he or she probably does. If drinking causes repeated disruptions in any aspect of a person's life and that person does not stop drinking, he or she is probably dependent on alcohol.

A person who is not dependent on alcohol will usually stop drinking, with or without help or treatment, once he or she realizes that the drinking is harming the family and other relationships. Due to the nature of the disease, an alcoholic will continue drinking even though it interferes with his or her important relationships.

There are many telltale signs of alcoholism. In the lists below you may find one or many signs that you can relate to. The signs apply to all stages of alcoholism. It is unlikely that all the signs are present in a single individual. Look hard for the signs that **do** apply. If only one applies there can still be a problem. Don't be fooled by the fact that each alcoholic has different telltale signs. The more telltale signs you or someone you care about has, the greater the chance that the individual has a drinking problem or is an alcoholic. The one thing alcoholics have in common is a loss of control over drinking and a consequent deterioration in their lives.

Because alcoholism develops slowly, it can take years to realize that you or someone you care about has a problem with drinking. Recognizing the signs is the first step to realizing that there is a problem and to stopping it. Remember, that it is not only alcoholics that need help but alcohol abusers too.

Early warning signs are:

- an increase in the FREQUENCY of drinking
- an increase in the AMOUNT of alcohol consumed
- an increase in the need to FEEL THE EFFECT of alcohol - to get intoxicated

Telltale signs in the early, middle and late stages:

- ❑ finding an excuse to drink
- ❑ finding non-drinking events boring

- drinking to build confidence with other people
- getting intoxicated when you or someone you care about planned not to
- drinking to relieve tension or to escape problems
- having trouble stopping after the first drink
- craving a drink at a certain time of the day
- finding it difficult to turn down the offer of a drink
- sneaking drinks
- gulping drinks (drinking very fast and often without mixers)
- drinking more and more to achieve the same effect
- having guilt feelings about one's drinking
- having feelings of remorse after drinking too much
- being on the defensive about one's drinking
- blaming others for drinking
- experiencing physical problems caused by drinking
- experiencing frequent, unpredictable mood swings
- trying to control drinking by changing types of alcohol
- hiding alcohol
- making promises to quit and then breaking them
- lying about one's drinking
- drinking in the morning to get rid of a hangover
- drinking at work
- drinking and driving
- skipping meals when drinking
- having blackouts (that is, not remembering what was said or done when intoxicated even though the drinker did not pass out)
- binge drinking
- having accidents at work or at home resulting in injury and/or damage to property
- neglecting family responsibilities
- missing days at work because of drinking

- being late for work because of drinking
- leaving work early on a regular basis to go drinking
- losing a job or nearly losing a job because of drinking
- showing a personality change when drinking
- missing planned family or social activities due to drinking
- family or friends commenting on the drinking
- a woman drinking during pregnancy
- being concerned about your drinking or the drinking of someone you care about
- refusing to discuss his or her drinking and/or discuss possibility that he or she might have a drinking problem

Did you find the above test a little overwhelming? Then take this short self-test:

Check your answers to the following questions:

	YES	NO
1. Do you or someone you care about lose time from work or miss appointments due to drinking?	❑	❑
2. Do you or someone you care about sometimes binge on alcohol?	❑	❑
3. Do you or someone you care about sometimes feel guilty about drinking?	❑	❑
4. Do you or someone you care about need more and more alcohol to become intoxicated?	❑	❑

5. Do you or someone you care about often regret things said or done while intoxicated? ❏ ❏

6. Do you or someone you care about suffer loss of memory (blackout) while or after drinking? ❏ ❏

7. Do you or someone you care about often fail to keep promises made to control or cut down on drinking? ❏ ❏

8. Do you or someone you care about find that drinking is harming, disrupting or worrying the family? ❏ ❏

9. Do you or someone you care about eat little or irregularly when drinking? ❏ ❏

10. Do you or someone you care about drink in the morning or "need" a drink to get over a hangover? ❏ ❏

11. Do you or someone you care about ever drive while intoxicated? ❏ ❏

A "yes" answer to one or more of the above questions indicates that you or someone you care about may be an alcoholic or on the road to becoming an alcoholic. Seek professional help. A professional trained in alcoholism will help you determine if you or someone you care about is an alcoholic and what you can do about it.

If you believe that the above is not enough to help you determine whether you or someone you care about is an alcoholic, you can turn to the *Appendix* for other tests used by physicians and professionals in the field of substance abuse to screen for alcohol problems.

A blackout is an important telltale sign. What is a blackout and how can I tell if someone is having a blackout?

A blackout is an alcohol-induced period of amnesia, not to be confused with passing out. A blackout can be likened to being unconscious yet fully awake. A person appears to everyone, including himself or herself, to be fully aware of what he or she is saying or doing and appears fully in control. A person can perform any activity during a blackout. A blackout may last for seconds, minutes, hours, or days. Following a blackout, however, the alcoholic will have no memory of what was said or done in that time period. Neither will they be able to recall the events at any later stage. Huge chunks of time can go unaccounted for as the alcoholism progresses.

There is no way to know if someone is experiencing a blackout. The drinker will realize only after the fact that he or she cannot recall events from the blackout period. Such realization usually arises from discussion of the events with other people. You will learn about the blackout only if the drinker admits to the blackout or by picking up cues from the drinker. For example, if, at a later stage, you are talking with the person who suffered a blackout and discuss something that he or she said or did in that time period. The drinker will usually be surprised, and possibly deny whatever it is you are talking about. A common situation occurs when a parent, having a blackout, promises something to his or her children and then has no recollection of the promise, and gets mad at them for their "false accusations."

Blackouts are very scary and are often the reason that an alcoholic will finally seek help. Waking up after a night on the town and not knowing how he or she got home or to bed, assuming he or she did make it to his or her own bed, can be very scary indeed.

You may think alcohol picks you up, but it will eventually let you down.

Anonymous

CHAPTER 4

The Physical Effects of Drinking

"You can die from drinking too much."

Drinking too much alcohol can kill you. Do you want to cut your life short? Think about what you could do with an "extra" ten to fifteen years, the average number of years for premature death from excessive drinking.

No part of your body escapes the effects of alcohol. Alcohol is a toxic drug; it is a poison to your body. When taken in large amounts over a period of time, alcohol will affect virtually every part of your body. Alcohol can have both short-term and long-term effects on the body.

What are the short-term effects of alcohol on the body?

Upset stomach	Ever felt queasy after a "night out"?
Diarrhea	Not necessarily caused by "something you ate"!
Anemia	The all too familiar "blahs" from too much partying!
Decreased fitness	Remember the hangovers! Hangovers are caused by the diuretic nature of alcohol. You're all dried out.
Skin problems	Alcohol is a diuretic causing the skin to dry out.

What are the long-term effects of drinking?

Unfortunately, the list of the long-term effects of drinking is long because the whole body is affected.

Another unfortunate fact is that little time is spent in medical school on the subject of alcohol abuse and alcoholism although the amount of time has increased in recent years. Therefore, if you lie about how much you drink, do not count on your doctor to figure out that you may have an alcohol problem or that the condition that prompted you to visit your doctor is caused by alcohol. Studies have shown that doctors fail to diagnose alcoholism in 90 percent of their alcoholic patients. Instead of treating the cause of your condition - your drinking - your doctor may treat your heart, liver or other conditions while you continue to poison and harm yourself with further drinking.

Remember from what you have read so far, that you cannot effectively treat the problems that the alcohol is causing, you have to treat the primary problem - your drinking.

If you do not stop drinking too much, the following are examples of physical conditions that may develop over a period of time:

Brain	Problems with attention, learning, cognition and memory.
	Premature aging of the brain.
	Wernicke-Korsakoff's syndrome - symptoms include short-term memory loss, disorientation and emotional disturbances.
Mouth and throat	Increased incidence of cancer.
Stomach	Ulcers.
	Gastritis - superficial, widespread inflammation of the stomach wall.
	Acid reflux.
Pancreas	Pancreatitis - inflammation of the pancreas.
	Increased incidence of cancer.
Liver	Fatty liver - fat deposits in the liver. Reversible with abstinence.
	Alcoholic hepatitis - inflammation of the liver. Reversible with abstinence.

Cirrhosis of the liver - scar tissue replaces normal liver tissue. Cirrhosis is the most advanced form of alcoholic liver injury and one of the top ten causes of death in the United States. It can stabilize with abstinence.

Liver cancer.

Heart and Vascular System

Heart muscle damage - cardiomyopathy.

Congestive heart failure.

Irregular heart rhythm - arrhythmia.

High blood pressure - hypertension.

Stroke.

Lungs

Increased susceptibility to pulmonary infection and pneumonia.

Reproductive System

Fetal alcohol syndrome. Maternal drinking, including even "social drinking" affects the developing fetus and can result in abnormalities and mental retardation of the newborn. The best advice for pregnant women continues to be abstinence. Your baby is at risk!

In men, heavy drinking impairs the production of sperm and testosterone and can lead to infertility and impotence. Women are at risk for

	menstrual irregularities and infertility.
Kidneys	Prolonged heavy drinking can lead to kidney failure.
Blood	Increase infection risks due to decreased production of white blood cells.
	Anemia - low red cell count.
	Impaired blood clotting, which increases the risk of stroke and heart attack.
Skin	Dilation of blood vessels.
	Reddened face and nose.
	Scaly skin.
Hormonal System	Alcohol alters critical hormonal balances that affect virtually the entire body.
	Sugar metabolism disturbances - hyperglycemia and hypoglycemia.
Immune System	Alcohol impairs the body's defenses against bacteria and viruses.
Musculoskeletal System	Increased risk of osteoporosis. Increased risk of fractures due to falling while intoxicated.
	Various forms of arthritis.
Miscellaneous effects	Malnutrition.
	Injuries from motor vehicle and other accidents.

Do you want any of the above to happen to you? No, of course not. If the drinking is not stopped or severely curtailed, however, then any one or more of the above can happen. You could die. Not a pleasant thought, is it?

There is nothing so bad that can happen to you that a drink won't make worse.

We are what we repeatedly do.

Aristotle

CHAPTER 5

Defenses Used by the Drinker

"They didn't serve dinner until 10 p.m. How was I meant to stay sober?"

What is a defense?

Basically, a defense is an excuse. The alcoholic, because of negative behavior caused by drinking, is vulnerable and open to criticism from relatives, friends and acquaintances. To protect himself or herself from feelings of guilt and paranoia, and to cope with day-to-day living, the alcoholic uses a series of defense mechanisms. The number and variety of defenses increase as the disease progresses.

Why do alcoholics use defenses?

Defenses help protect alcoholics from being hurt. Defenses help to reduce alcoholics' anxiety in the short term because, to alcoholics, defenses explain away the negative aspects of their behavior and justify their drinking.

Defenses reduce the chances that alcoholics will do anything positive about their drinking problem because defenses block the ability to see and experience reality. Alcoholics perceive events the way they want to. Their perception can be so distorted that you may wonder if you were at the same event that the alcoholic described, even though you were!

What are some examples of defenses?

Denial

Denial is the most commonly used defense. By denying anything related to their drinking - often the fact that they drink - alcoholics can protect themselves from pain and hurt.

Examples

"I don't care what you or anyone else thinks, I am not an alcoholic."

"Your blood tests must be wrong, I don't drink."

" I don't know whose bottles those are in my car, I told you I have given up drinking."

" What's the big deal? My drinking affects only me."

" I'm doing my job. Don't bug me about my drinking."

" I never did that, it must have been someone else."

"I have no idea what you are talking about. I didn't say that."

Rationalization

Alcoholics justify their drinking, how much they drink and what happens while they are intoxicated.

Examples

"Drinking is part of my job." (It is?)

"If I wasn't so tired and depressed the drinks wouldn't have hit me so hard."

"Mike was pouring strong drinks. Everyone got a little drunk."

" Everyone gets high at weddings."

" I **need** alcohol to help me sleep (to calm me down, to relax me)."

"Alcohol is the only thing that relieves my stress."

" If I had a problem with alcohol my doctor would have told me to stop."

"Drinking is part of my lifestyle."

Externalization

Alcoholics often blame others - in fact, anybody - for drinking too much, for their problems and for their bad behavior. Anything to try and justify their drinking and bad behavior. The drinking, the alcoholic believes, is because of other problems in life.

Examples

"If **you** didn't nag so much, I wouldn't drink."

" My job is so frustrating."

" My boss is giving me a hard time."

" Being married to you is enough to make anyone drink."

" With all my worries, you'd drink too."

" Of course I drink, how else can I shut out the noise of the kids."

" Drinking is the only way I can cope with our marriage problems."

Minimizing

Alcoholics attempt to minimize an event until it seems insignificant. Alcoholics minimize the amount they drink and the consequences of their drinking.

Examples

"I think you're overreacting to all this."

" Okay, so I had one or two drinks but it was only a small accident." (This in response to the reality of a high blood alcohol content and a totaled car!)

" No, I only screamed at her." (This in response to an obvious and witnessed beating of a spouse.)

Selective Recall

Alcoholics only remember what they want to remember about a situation - those facts that will support their view and justify their behavior.

Example

"How could I hurt John's feelings? He offered to drive me home and I didn't want to offend him." (This in response to the reality of being so intoxicated that John had to drive his friend home.)

Euphoric Recall

Alcoholics often only recall the good in a situation. Alcoholics remember that they were the "life and soul of the party" but not how drunk and embarrassing they were. Alcoholics only remember how good the alcohol made them feel.

Repression

Who wants to remember something that made them feel pain, shame, guilt, scared, embarrassed or angry? Sometimes it seems easier to just "forget" what really happened or what was felt than to deal with it. Alcoholics literally shut their embarrassing and shameful behavior out of their minds.

Example

After a night out, alcoholics on waking would rather "forget" what happened the night before because it is too uncomfortable to think about.

Hostile Silence

The alcoholic simply refuses to discuss his or her drinking and will often just leave a room when the subject is raised.

Indignation

The alcoholic taps into the guilt of the person mentioning his or her drinking and responds with such indignation as to induce silence.

Example

"What do you mean you went to see a counselor about my drinking. How could you go to a stranger behind my back?"

"How can you humiliate me like this in front of everyone?"

"How can you criticize my drinking, you also drink."

Men are born to succeed, not to fail.

Henry David Thoreau

CHAPTER 6

Enabling: How We Support the Drinking

"Oh, but she doesn't drink on Wednesdays when her mother comes to dinner."

What is enabling?

Enabling is the behavior of others that protects the alcoholic from the consequences of his or her drinking and allows the alcoholic to continue drinking.

What is an enabler?

A person who enables, or assists, is an enabler. An enabler defends the alcoholic's drinking to everyone but the alcoholic. The enabler uses the same "defenses" to the rest of the world that the alcoholic uses.

Without the support of an enabler, the alcoholic would find it difficult to continue drinking. Enabling behavior prevents both the enabler and the alcoholic from seeing the reality of the situation.

Who can be an enabler?

An enabler is anyone who covers up for the alcoholic's behavior. Enablers can be spouses, children, parents, friends, co-workers, neighbors, bosses, employees, doctors, nurses, clergy, psychiatrists, psychologists, social workers, teachers, police officers, lawyers and judges.

A primary enabler is a person whose cooperation is often essential to the alcoholic's continued drinking. A primary enabler is usually the one who protects both the alcoholic and other family members from the negative effects of the disease. If the primary enabler alters his or her behavior the alcoholic would probably have to face the consequences of the drinking and be forced to change because the primary enabler is no longer "fixing things."

A secondary enabler plays a less dramatic role in perpetuating the alcoholic's drinking. The alcoholic's employer is often a secondary enabler. The secondary enabler tends to reinforce the alcoholic's pattern of denial by not addressing the drinking or turning a "blind eye." The alcoholic is then left with the impression that his or her drinking cannot be all that bad because if it was, people would surely say something!

What is some enabling behavior?

1. Lying to family and friends about the alcoholic's drinking.

2. Making excuses for problems caused by the alcoholic's drinking.

3. Lying to the alcoholic's employer about drinking.

4. Taking on the alcoholic's responsibilities - for example, financial responsibilities.

5. Taking care of the alcoholic physically.

6. Ignoring the pain and hurt of the children.

7. Avoiding conflict with the alcoholic by "accepting" his or her excuses.

8. Not following through on the advice obtained from counselors or knowledgeable friends - those trying to help. And, not getting help.

9. Drinking with the alcoholic in the hope of keeping the drinking within limits.

10. Getting the alcoholic out of financial or legal trouble.

Why do people enable?

People enable because they think that they are protecting themselves, people they care about or the alcoholic. Those enablers who are living with an alcoholic enable to hide all the problems that can come with living in an alcoholic family - for example, financial troubles, delinquency, child or spouse abuse. People enable to hide their feelings of guilt, shame, inadequacy, insecurity, and resentment caused by the alcoholic's drinking.

Why must I change my enabling behavior?

If you do not change, there is little chance that the alcoholic will change. You want to get the alcoholic to treatment and to stop drinking. Changing your enabling behavior is a step in the right direction.

Everyone is affected by the drinking and gets trapped in the same emotional chaos as the alcoholic. You cannot do anything for the alcoholic unless you do something for yourself first. You need to take action. It is important to realize that you have been supporting the alcoholic's drinking and that if you change, then the alcoholic will be encouraged and forced to make changes too. The alcoholic is dependent on his or her enablers to support or maintain his or her drinking. The alcoholic is more dependent on you than you are on him or her. Without you, drinking would be more difficult to maintain. It follows, therefore, that a radical change in your enabling behavior could force the alcoholic to change and seek help. All your enabling behavior never got the alcoholic to stop drinking in the past; don't kid yourself that enabling behavior will cause a change in the future.

For those of you who live with an alcoholic, changing the enabling behavior can be frightening because you have been around the drinking for so long. A change, however, cannot be worse than what you have lived through already. If you cannot change the alcoholic - and how you have probably tried - then change yourself. Why should you be dragged down with the alcoholic?

Another reason to change your enabling behavior is to prevent a disaster from occurring. You need to face your denial, to realize the severity of the problem before the alcoholic resorts to violence such as killing or injuring a person while driving intoxicated, setting fire to personal property, using a firearm while intoxicated or resorting to domestic violence or child abuse.

What can I do to change my enabling behavior?

1. Face the truth - see the reality of the situation and that the alcoholic needs outside help.

2. Learn about the disease of alcoholism. You can let the alcoholic know you are doing this.

3. Get help for yourself from someone you trust - a professional counselor trained in alcoholism, a knowledgeable friend, social worker, clergy or Al-Anon, which is a support group for the family and friends of alcoholics. Living with the effects of someone else's drinking can be devastating and difficult to bear without help. Treat your own problems related to the drinking. Make yourself well!

4. Identify you enabling behaviors.

5. Learn how to stop your enabling behaviors.

6. Stop focusing on the alcoholic and the problems that drinking causes.

7. Understand and practice controlling your emotions which are probably chaotic as a result of being around

an alcoholic. Try to remain calm and factually honest when speaking about the alcoholic's behavior and its day-to-day consequences.

8. Create a healthy home environment. Where appropriate, explain the disease of alcoholism to family members including children. Let them know that alcoholism is a disease and that no individual or event cause it. Try to include the alcoholic in family life.

9. Pursue other interests outside the home to take your focus off the alcoholic.

10. Stay put. Don't make a geographic change. Alcohol is everywhere. Moving to another part of the town, state or country will only help the alcoholic to continue his or her denial and allow the drinking to continue. It is not where you live that makes him or her drink!

11. Never ride with a drunk driver and do not allow anyone else to ride with the drunk driver. You may not be able to stop the drinker from driving, but you can stop yourself, your children or others from riding with a drinker. Drunk drivers, even if they are loved ones, pose life threatening situations every minute they are behind the wheel.

12. Let crises happen if it is the natural course of events. Don't pick up the pieces as the alcoholic's life falls apart. Don't feel sorry for him or her. Make no more excuses for the alcoholic. One crisis too many may be the straw that "breaks alcoholic's back" and gets him or her to seek help.

13. Be gentle on yourself - you are not the cause of the alcoholism. Be patient and live one day at a time.

Alcoholism takes a long time to develop and recovery does not occur overnight. Try to accept that setbacks and relapses will occur and react as calmly as possible.

Changing your enabling behavior is not an easy task because, as with the alcoholism, it took years to develop and will require constant vigilance on your behalf to change. It is an effort well worth undertaking and essential to the sanity and survival of all parties affected by the alcoholism.

What can happen if I change my enabling behavior?

You will be a lot happier, feel in greater control of your life and you may achieve what you have wanted all along - to get the drinking to stop.

With the collapse of the drinker's enabling system the drinker has to take responsibility for his or her drinking actions. There is no one left to pick up the pieces or to blame for the chaos in his or her life.

Changing your enabling behavior will give you the strength and resolve to undertake an Intervention - discussed in the chapter on *Intervention: Something More You Can Do to Help* - if that is what you need to do to get the alcoholic to treatment. As an enabler you are only keeping the alcoholic closer to the bottle. Free of your enabling behavior, the alcoholic has more chance of getting to treatment.

Alcoholism isn't a spectator sport.
Eventually the whole family gets to play.

Rebeta-Burditt

CHAPTER 7

17 Don'ts: If Someone You Care About is Dependent on Alcohol

Don't listen to, "if you loved me, you would call the office and say I'm sick!"

You can help someone you care about take responsibility for the drinking and his or her own life by following these 17 Don'ts:

> 1. Don't see alcoholism as a family disgrace. It is a disease and, as with other diseases, recovery is possible. Remember, no one wants to become an alcoholic.

2. Don't hide or dump bottles or shelter the alcoholic from situations where alcohol is present. The alcoholic will find other ways to get a drink.

3. Don't drink along with the alcoholic. It will not make the alcoholic drink less or get closer to seeking help. By also drinking you reinforce and condone the habit and keep the alcoholic from seeking help for himself or herself.

4. Don't give the alcoholic responsibilities or duties and then get angry when they are not met or accomplished.

5. Don't treat the alcoholic like a child. You would not do so if he or she were suffering from some other disease.

6. Don't punish, nag, bribe or preach to the alcoholic. Such actions only increase the alcoholic's guilt, self-hatred, self-pity and resentment and push him or her closer to the bottle. Such actions also cause the alcoholic to lie or to make promises that cannot be kept.

7. Don't be fooled by apparent lulls in the drinking. By going "on the wagon" for a while, the alcoholic may be trying to convince you that he or she does not have a drinking problem. Things may get better during a non-drinking period but the situation will deteriorate when the drinking inevitably starts again.

8. Don't threaten the alcoholic unless you intend to carry out the threat. If you don't carry out the threat, the alcoholic will learn that you don't mean what you say.

9. Don't cover up or make excuses for the alcoholic. Protecting the alcoholic from the consequences of drinking will only keep him or her from seeking help.

10. Don't take on the alcoholic's responsibilities. He or she needs to face the problems caused by his or her drinking, try to solve them or face the consequences. Taking over responsibilities from alcoholics reduces their self esteem and dignity, which leaves them feeling unworthy, unneeded and unwanted.

11. Don't get into arguments when the alcoholic has been drinking. Neither of you can win when "crazy-making alcohol" is talking.

12. Don't demand or accept unreasonable promises from the alcoholic. Don't use the "if you loved me" routine. The alcoholic has a disease. The alcoholic has no control over drinking and the nature of the disease will sabotage any promises made. A broken promise will lead to more lies and distrust.

13. Don't try to protect the alcoholic from danger. Alcoholics have got to face the consequences of their drinking or else they will never get the help they need. An exception can be made, however, when the danger is drunk driving in which case it would be appropriate to take all reasonable steps possible to stop the drinker from driving.

14. Don't get or listen to advice from friends who do not understand the disease of alcoholism. Conflicting, inconsistent and incorrect information will make you more confused and desperate. Get help from someone trained in alcoholism.

15. Don't try to handle the alcoholic and the alcoholism yourself. You cannot do it alone. Get help from a professional trained in alcoholism for both the alcoholic and yourself.

16. Don't feel guilty or responsible for the alcoholic's behavior. You did not cause the alcoholic to drink, you cannot control his or her drinking and you cannot cure his or her drinking.

17. Don't forget to look after yourself and let the alcoholic look after himself or herself.

Although the world is full of suffering, it is also full of the overcoming of it.

Helen Keller

CHAPTER 8

Intervention: Something More You Can Do to Help

"You can love someone to death. If you don't intervene they could die."

You feel that you have tried everything to get the person you care about to seek help for his or her drinking. You have changed your enabling behavior and the drinker is still not motivated to seek help. You feel you cannot cope anymore or bear to watch the person you care about drink himself or herself to death. The person you care about still does not admit to having a drinking problem. You are getting desperate! You want to take some action to prevent the drinking from becoming any more destructive than it already is.

There is something you can do - an Intervention.

What is an Intervention?

An Intervention is where a group of concerned people meet the alcoholic face to face with the goal of getting the alcoholic to be evaluated by a professional trained in alcoholism and following through on the recommendation of the evaluation.

An Intervention is a loving, caring, and well-rehearsed way of telling the alcoholic, in a group setting, the extent to which the drinking is affecting his or her life, as well as your own. The alcoholic is offered a set of consequences that all lead to his or her evaluation at a treatment center and the acceptance of some kind of treatment - the first step to recovery.

Intervention can be seen as creating a controlled crisis in an attempt to get the alcoholic to treatment.

Why do an Intervention?

Because nothing else has worked to get the alcoholic to seek help for his or her drinking! And, Intervention has a very good track record; many Interventions succeed in getting an alcoholic to treatment.

The person you care about has a progressive disease and is physically and emotionally sick. All of his or her behavior is governed by drinking. He or she has no control over drinking - drinking controls him or her. The person you care about is unable to help himself or herself. The drinking problem will not go away by itself. Through an Intervention you can take action before a crisis occurs. Why wait until a crisis occurs? The sooner you can get an alcoholic to treatment, the greater the chance of achieving sobriety.

If you do **not** do an Intervention, the person you care about could die from drinking.

Who initiates an Intervention?

Any concerned person can initiate an Intervention - a spouse, a child, a parent, a friend, an employer, an employee.

Do I have a right to Intervene?

You sure do!

An Intervention is a loving, caring act. The alcoholic has no control over drinking and what it is doing to him or her. The person you care about did not choose to become an alcoholic and deserves a chance at being freed from the bottle.

By intervening you are offering your spouse, friend, parent, child, employee or whomever, help: as a way to avoid death from drinking. If he or she will not seek help, then you can offer freedom through Intervention. If he or she refuses the help you offer at the Intervention then that is his or her responsibility. You will have done everything within your power to help.

As hard as an Intervention can be to undertake, it is a profound gift of love and an important step in treating the alcoholism.

Who is involved in an Intervention?

Concerned family members and friends with the guidance of a professional, someone who is trained to do an

Intervention, are involved. Family and friends who have the greatest influence in the alcoholic's life and those who have the strongest consequences to impose are the most effective in an Intervention.

A boss or co-worker is sometimes involved because losing a job is often more threatening to the alcoholic than losing family or possessions.

What steps do I take to prepare for an Intervention?

1. Seek the assistance of a professional counselor who is trained in Intervention. Intervention can be a difficult process, burdened with emotions, fears, guilt and resentment. Have a professional help you prepare and be present during the Intervention. It is important to be well prepared and focused because there is much at stake in the Intervention.

It must be stressed that, while it is recommended to have a professional counselor present at the Intervention, it is by no means imperative. Anyone who is sincere about wanting to help an alcoholic, can help and be successful in reaching the goal of getting the alcoholic to treatment.

To find a counselor, read the chapter on *Where to Find Help* - the centers and state agencies listed should be able to provide you with a list of counselors in your area.

2. Select the Intervention team. Ideally, the team should be comprised of two or more people. A team size of three to five people seems to be most effective. No one who has a drinking problem should be allowed on the Intervention team.

3. Select a neutral place to undertake the Intervention.

4. Learn about the process of Intervention. Read the books recommended in *Suggested Reading* which deal specifically with Intervention. The books will take you through an Intervention step by step. Watch a video of a dramatized Intervention to get the feel for it and whether you still want to be part of it.

5. Prepare, in writing, what you are going to say and determine the consequences you are going to present to the alcoholic if he or she does not enter treatment. Each member of the team needs to do this. Two powerful consequences are threat of divorce and the loss of a job. You must be prepared to follow through with your threat if the Intervention is to succeed.

6. Make arrangements for treatment. See chapters on *Treatment* and *Where to Find Help*. It is important that the arrangements for treatment are made before the Intervention so that the alcoholic can go **directly** to treatment from the Intervention - before he or she can think of an excuse why not to go!

7. Rehearse the Intervention. This allows for members of the Intervention team to rehearse what they are going to say in a group setting. It is important to remember that you are trying to offer the person you care about a solution to his or her drinking. Express yourself with love and caring. The alcoholic thrives on confrontation. Love has the best shot of breaking resistance.

Understand that you will probably feel guilt and anger which is quite normal. Try your best, however, to keep your emotions in check while undertaking the Intervention. By doing so, you will increase your chance of success of getting the person you care about to treatment. As hard as it is, you need to detach to allow the loving and caring to come through.

8. Do the Intervention. Having selected a time and place that will surprise the alcoholic and will have him or her as sober as possible, he or she walks into a roomful of concerned people and the Intervention begins.

No matter how emotional the Intervention is, the alcoholic should not be allowed physical contact with any member of the Intervention team until he or she has agreed to enter treatment. If the Intervention proceeds without interruption, the last person to speak offers the options to be presented to the alcoholic: to be professionally evaluated at a treatment center and follow through with the recommended treatment or face the consequences that have been given.

At this point, the alcoholic will either accept without protest your recommendations or embark on the pattern of denials. This is the time to break through any denials with facts of the disease and how his or her behavior does not match the denials. Do not bargain! Then, at this point, the alcoholic may realize that the "game" of denials is over and that he or she has no option but to accept your offer of help and treatment.

How long does an Intervention take?

Interventions last approximately 30-60 minutes, until the group has reached the goal of getting the alcoholic to agree to be evaluated at a treatment center or realize that the group will not achieve the goal that day.

Why does Intervention work?

Being surprised by a roomful of concerned people who express with love the extent to which his or her drinking is affecting everybody, the alcoholic is moved to take action to stop the drinking. There is little room for argument and the consequences offered - loss of family, job and anything else precious - do not seem too appealing! During the Intervention, the alcoholic finally realizes how his or her life is being affected by the drinking and that if help is not sought, alcohol may be all he or she has left.

What if the Intervention fails?

It cannot fail. The goal of getting the alcoholic to treatment may not have been reached but the secret is out. All involved in the Intervention have a new awareness and will not be able to play games any longer. No one around the alcoholic will be able to retreat into denial again.

Can you do another Intervention if the initial Intervention does not achieve your goal?

Absolutely. The alcoholic still needs your help and their life is still in danger. After the initial Intervention, the weakened defense mechanisms of the alcoholic make it easier to succeed on a second or even third Intervention attempt.

Why don't more people do an Intervention?

Simply - they don't know about it! Or, how it works.

"Intervention can save a life, a family, a friendship."

You may be disappointed if you fail, but you are doomed if you don't try.

Beverly Sills

CHAPTER 9

Treatment: The Types of Help Available

"Reach out for help, not a drink."

There are many treatment options for alcohol abusers and alcoholics. There is help available to assist in achieving sobriety. There are treatment centers opening up every day. There are more counselors being trained to address alcohol abuse and alcoholism each year, there are more doctors who have increased their knowledge of the disease, and there are new support groups forming daily around the country. The federal and state governments are spending more on stopping the swelling tide of alcohol abuse and alcoholism, disseminating information to opening new treatment centers. There **is** help out there.

Each person has different needs. Keep looking until you find a treatment program that suits you or the person you care about. After all the pain and suffering that the drinking has already caused, it is worth spending the time to find the best treatment for you and the person you care about.

Recovery from any disease, including alcoholism, is not instantaneous. Overnight miracles are not likely to occur. The body, mind, emotions and spirit all need time to repair from a disease that has been causing damage for years. The whole body is sick and will take time to heal. Be patient and persistent, recovery is possible.

What types of treatment are there available?

Treatment can take many forms due to the different needs of each alcohol abuser or alcoholic. Treatment is available in alcoholism units within hospitals; private clinics designed specifically for the care of alcoholics; residential alcohol rehabilitation centers; self-help support groups such as Alcoholics Anonymous, Rational Recovery, Secular Organizations for Sobriety, and Women for Sobriety; and, private practitioners such as alcoholism counselors, psychologists, psychiatrists and social workers.

Specialized alcohol treatment centers generally offer the best treatment choice as they have been designed specifically for the treatment of alcoholics, with staff trained in the disease of alcoholism. The type of treatment chosen will be dependent on the severity of the drinking problem.

Do all alcohol abusers and alcoholics have to be treated as an inpatient?

No, but it can improve the chances of recovery.

Alcohol abusers and many alcoholics in the early stages of alcoholism can be treated successfully as outpatients, allowing them to remain at home and work while receiving treatment. Other alcohol abusers and early stage alcoholics have found sobriety by just attending a support group such as Alcoholics Anonymous, Rational Recovery, Secular Organizations For Sobriety, or Women For Sobriety.

Some alcohol abusers and early stage alcoholics find that an inpatient setting provides the discipline in which to stop drinking and get the emotional, mental, physical and spiritual support needed as they lose their "crutch": alcohol. The inpatient setting provides a medically-supervised alcohol-free environment in which the alcohol abuser and alcoholic is given the opportunity to rest and obtain the proper nutrition needed for healing from years of abuse.

Some alcohol abusers have successfully stopped or reduced their drinking without participation in formal treatment programs. Alcohol abusers have also responded well to Interventions. Brief counseling and strong social support may be all he or she needs to stop drinking. If these methods are not successful, the alcohol abuser can always try different or more intensive treatment.

Inpatient treatment is recommended for middle stage alcoholics and strongly recommended for those who are in need of medical attention, are in the late stages of the disease and need supervised withdrawal, or are in any way unable to care for themselves.

Are all treatment centers the same?

No. There are centers opening up all over the country in response to the growing awareness of alcohol abuse and alcoholism. Be very wary of any "quick cure" center. It is important to check the credentials of the center and make sure they have a program suited to you and the alcoholic.

If for financial, geographic or other personal reasons you cannot attend your first choice of treatment center, choose the one that most closely matches your ideal.

What should you look for in a treatment center's program?

It is advisable to select a program that:

1. Acknowledges that alcoholism is a disease - a disease that can be halted but not cured. The program should also be based on the premise that optimal recovery is dependent on total and continuous abstinence from alcohol or substitute drugs.

2. Incorporates nutrition into the program. This is essential to successful treatment and to long term sobriety.

3. Educates the alcoholic and family about the disease of alcoholism and how to handle life without alcohol.

4. Has a staff that is experienced in the treatment of alcoholism.

5. Has group counseling.

6. Involves the family in treatment and follow-up care.

7. Has thorough follow-up care and monitors progress.

8. Recommends support group participation to assist in long-term sobriety.

The treatment center should allow you to tour the facility without obligation. The center should also answer any questions you may have, such as success rate, costs, length of treatment and whether detoxification facilities are available.

If you are looking for a treatment center that is suitable for a child you will need to ask some specific questions such as whether they have an adolescent treatment program, whether parents can visit the center and whether they have a school or tutorial program. It is important to establish that a center caters to the special needs of adolescents. If in doubt, keep looking.

Who will pay for the treatment?

Most medical insurance companies pay for treatment. Call the Admissions Office of the treatment center to determine whether you are covered or not.

Why is total abstinence so important?

Alcoholics have no control over drinking. There is no such thing as "just one drink." For the alcoholic there is **always** the possibility of relapse. Although abstinence is demanding and requires constant vigilance, sobriety is easier for the alcoholic to achieve than any other solution.

Why is nutrition so important?

Most alcoholics, due to years of drinking, suffer from malnutrition. Alcoholics tend to eat poorly, often eating less than the amounts necessary to provide sufficient carbohydrates, protein, fats, vitamins and minerals. Some alcoholics ingest as much as 50 percent of their total daily calories from alcohol! Chronic heavy drinkers are deficient in many essential vitamins and minerals. Not only do alcoholics eat poorly but their bodies do not efficiently absorb what they eat. Many alcoholics also suffer from hypoglycemia - low blood sugar - which can be treated with good nutrition.

Nutrition is a critical ingredient to assuring successful treatment and restoring the body's chemical balance. The alcoholic needs vitamins and mineral supplements to repair the damage caused to his or her body from years of drinking. It is imperative that part of the treatment program is devoted to repairing the physical damage caused by drinking. All the psychological treatment in the world will not give the body its much needed nutrients.

Alcoholism is a physical disease that damages the mind, emotions, spirit and body. All, therefore, need to be treated to assure optimum recovery and a return to good health. The alcoholic not only wants to get sober but healthy too. A strict nutrition regime is an important step in helping the body recover from years of drinking.

Do the family or I need to get treatment?

Yes. Alcoholism is a family disease and anyone who has lived with the alcoholic has been affected emotionally and psychologically. The family needs to get help at the same time as the alcoholic in order to prepare for the changes that will occur in a household of a recovering alcoholic.

Your life has revolved around the drinking almost as much as the alcoholic's. If the person you care about stops drinking, your life will alter too. Be prepared! Go to Al-Anon, other support groups or individual therapy. The world as it existed, however awful, will change and the entire household will need to adapt. Even family members who are not living with the alcoholic have been affected and are advised to get treatment.

What is Alcoholics Anonymous (AA) and what are some of its principles?

1. AA is a group of recovering alcoholics who help each other stay sober.

2. AA offers to help anyone with a drinking problem.

The only requirement for AA membership is a desire to stop drinking.

3. Because all AA members are alcoholics, they have a special understanding of each other. AA provides ongoing help, advice and support.

4. AA encourages new members to abstain from drinking one day at a time. This approach makes the task of maintaining sobriety easier. AA members learn to concentrate on avoiding only one drink: the first one.

5. In AA you are accepted for who you are, not what you do. You are all equal in AA.

6. AA allows you to keep you anonymity, if that is what you want, and does not ask you to join anything or sign anything.

7. AA is not a religious organization and is not affiliated with any sect, denomination, politics, organization or institution.

8. AA has groups all over the world, which makes it easier for recovering alcoholics to travel knowing they can get support if needed.

9. AA has designed an effective Twelve Step Program to help in recovery.

10. AA is free and proven to be an effective part of treatment.

As with other forms of treatment, find an AA group that is best suited to your temperament and background and in which you feel most comfortable. Go to different groups for variety. Do what is best for your recovery. This advice is also applicable to the support groups discussed in the next question.

What are some of the other support groups available and what are their principles?

Until recently, AA was the only option for recovering alcoholics. Some alcoholics, however, found that AA did not suit their specific needs and founded their own support groups. These groups, as with AA, are free. The only requirement for joining is a desire to stop drinking. Abstinence is their goal. The three support groups discussed here - Rational Recovery, Secular Organizations for Sobriety and Women for Sobriety - appear to have filled a need because their membership has been growing yearly.

Rational Recovery (RR)

1. RR teaches that what leads to persistent drinking is a belief in your own powerlessness and incompetence.

2. Meetings do not follow a specific format. The discussions center on helping people recognize their addiction and how to overcome it.

3. Groups are generally limited to fourteen people.

4. A professional adviser - a medical doctor, psychiatrist, psychologist, social worker or nurse - attends each meeting and acts as a resource and sometimes moderates meetings.

5. RR members are encouraged to attend no more than two meetings per week in order to prevent an undesirable dependency on the group.

6. RR encourages members to move away from attending meetings and to become independent of the support group within a year.

Secular Organizations for Sobriety (SOS)

1. Focuses on self empowerment, self responsibility and human support.

2. SOS does not have a strict philosophy. Rather SOS deals with alcoholism by taking events one day at a time.

3. Each group is autonomous and holds meetings in the way that best suits the members' needs.

4. SOS believes that religion and sobriety are separate issues.

5. Each group has a maximum of twenty people who take turns acting as moderator.

6. Meetings consist of general discussions and are open to nonalcoholic family members and friends.

7. SOS encourages members to attend at least one meeting a week for the first six months and then on an "as needed" basis.

Women for Sobriety (WFS)

1. WFS was founded to specifically serve the needs of women alcoholics.

2. WFS meetings are moderated by former alcoholics who have been sober for at least one year and who have been trained in the principles of WFS.

3. WFS's program is based on Thirteen Acceptance Statements.

4. Members talk about personal problems related to recovery, or one of the Thirteen Acceptance Statements.

5. WFS's meeting size is generally limited to ten people with meetings once a week.

Is attending a support group important?

Attending support group meetings greatly enhances the chances of the alcoholic remaining sober over an extended period. Support groups provide the ongoing follow-up care needed for staying sober and are readily accessible to every alcoholic. The knowledge that other people have gone through the same experiences as the alcoholic can be a strength and a comfort - the alcoholic is not alone.

Attending a support group reinforces the alcoholic's commitment to his or her recovery - to changing and improving his or her quality of life.

How important is the alcoholic's commitment to treatment and recovery?

It is imperative. The alcoholic needs to accept responsibility for his or her own recovery. If the alcoholic's recovery is dependent on someone else - for example, to remind him or her to go to support group meetings, to take him or her to support group meetings or to cook nutritious meals - the alcoholic is jeopardizing the chances of a sustained recovery. The alcoholic needs to live life differently than before entering treatment and acknowledge that he or she can never safely take a drink.

Can a relapse happen if the alcoholic has had treatment?

Yes. Although the alcoholic is committed to recovery, he or she can still have a relapse. A relapse does not mean that the treatment has failed. As with other diseases, setbacks do occur. Sometimes a relapse convinces the alcoholic that abstinence is the only way to handle the disease.

Can drugs be used to treat alcoholics who repeatedly relapse?

Drug treatment for alcoholism is an ongoing area of research and the results have not been conclusive. To date, the drug naltrexone which was approved by the US Food and Drug Administration in 1994 and was the first drug approved for the treatment of alcoholism in nearly 50 years, has been found in some studies to cut relapse rates by up to 50 percent. With this approval, the use of drugs to treat alcoholism is likely to increase.

In consultation with a health care provider, the alcoholic needs to do what is best for his or her recovery. Naltrexone may be what is needed to help the alcoholic from repeated relapses.

Where do I find treatment centers, Alcoholics Anonymous and the other support groups?

Turn to the chapter on *Where to Find Help* and you will find addresses and telephone numbers for treatment centers and other help programs nationally and in your state.

You can also look in the telephone book under "Alcoholism" for further listings and for your local Alcoholics Anonymous, Al-Anon and other support groups.

Remember, alcoholism is a treatable disease. There is no need to suffer any more. Seek the help you or someone you care about deserve. You are not alone. Recovery is possible. Enjoy the journey to sobriety.

Good luck!

"There is a way to control alcoholism. Total abstinence"

It is common sense to take a method and try it.
If it fails, admit it frankly and try another.
But above all, try something.

Franklin D. Roosevelt

CHAPTER 10

General Questions and Answers

This chapter addresses questions that do not fall under one of the specific chapter headings and answers questions from readers of earlier editions of this book.

Is there any connection between smoking and drinking?

Research has shown that between 80 percent and 95 percent of alcoholics smoke cigarettes, a rate that is three times higher than among the population as a whole. It appears, too, that teens who begin smoking are three times more likely to begin using alcohol. Also, smokers are ten times more likely to develop alcoholism than are nonsmokers.

Smoking and drinking also complicate the physical ramifications. The risks of cancer of the mouth, throat and esophagus for the smoking drinker increase dramatically than if these two drugs are used individually. In short, being a drinker and a smoker increases your risk of cancer.

Smoking and drinking can also be a fire hazard. A drinker who passes out or falls asleep with a cigarette in hand can cause house fires or set fire to other personal property.

What is the relationship between alcohol and sleep?

The use of alcohol before going to sleep can disrupt normal sleep patterns and help create or aggravate sleep disorders, such as sleep apnea. Many people falsely use alcohol as a sedative to help them sleep. They may fall asleep more readily but their later sleeping hours will be fitful, leading to increased fatigue the following day.

When a person is sleep deprived and tired, alcohol affects the body more readily. Consider this scenario: It is Friday evening, after a tough week at work, Paul and Julia decide to go for a few drinks on the way home. Paul says, "I'll have only one drink as I'm so tired." When sleep deprived, however, one drink can be equal to four to six drinks. On the drive home, Paul has now become a double menace on the road - a sleep-deprived and alcohol-impaired driver even though his blood alcohol content (BAC) would be within legal limits.

Is there a problem with using alcohol as a tranquilizer to relieve stress?

Yes. When using alcohol as a tranquilizer for stress it is easy to consume more alcohol than is needed to provide a tranquilizing effect - to go from a therapeutic range to a toxic range. There are healthier methods, such as exercise, talking to friends, watching a movie or meditation, that will help relieve stress.

Anyone who has a problem with alcohol or is an alcoholic must not use alcohol to relieve stress because such use will aggravate existing problems and cause an alcoholic to sink deeper into his or her disease. Drinking will only cause more stress which then creates a vicious cycle.

Is there any relationship between suicide and drinking?

Alcohol abuse is often a contributing factor to suicide. The use of alcohol may reduce inhibitions and impair the judgment of someone contemplating suicide making the act more likely. Studies have shown that about 90 percent of alcoholics who commit suicide had been drinking prior to taking their lives, and over two thirds of attempted suicides involve frequent alcohol use.

Recent studies suggest that alcohol tends to be associated with impulsive rather than premeditated suicides - a sound reason for not having a gun in an alcoholic's household or car.

Does drinking make a person more aggressive or violent?

Studies have shown that alcohol alone does not cause violent behavior but may increase the risk of violent behavior for certain individuals. Environmental and cultural influences play a role in increased aggression with alcohol use for some people.

Recent studies show the following percentages of violent offenders who were drinking at the time of the offense and clearly illustrate an alcohol-violence association: up to 87 percent of homicide offenders, 37 percent of assault offenders, 60 percent of sexual offenders, up to 57 percent of men and 27 percent of women involved in marital violence, and 13 percent of child abusers had alcohol in their blood at the time of the offense.

Is there a relationship between domestic violence and drinking?

Yes. Studies of domestic violence indicate a high use of alcohol. Expanding on the previous question, studies have shown that rates of domestic violence are almost 15 times higher in households where the abuser is regularly drunk as opposed to never drunk. There also appears to be a strong link between alcoholism and child abuse, including incest. Studies have also shown that the person who has been abused stands a higher probability of abusing alcohol over time.

Drinking impairs judgment and reduces inhibitions which can lead to explosive situations in individuals prone to violence or in a confrontational or conflicting domestic situation. Domestic violence and alcohol can be a lethal combination and must be taken very seriously. The abused needs to seek help - no one has to put up with being abused.

What is the relationship between risky sexual behavior and drinking?

There is a definite relationship between alcohol use and risky sexual behavior, and it is not a positive one. The likelihood of engaging in casual sexual activity after drinking is far higher than when sober, particularly with a partner whom the alcoholic would not consider having sex with while sober. Being under the influence of alcohol impairs judgment about sex and contraception, creating increased risks for unplanned and unwanted pregnancy, sexual assault (rape, including date rape), or infection with a sexually transmitted disease, exposure to HIV and of developing AIDS. An alcoholic whose immune system has been weakened is at even greater risk.

Are there any particular concerns for older people and drinking?

Yes. Alcohol problems among the elderly often go undetected because the manifestations are mistaken for other conditions associated with aging. Because many elderly drinkers live alone, alcohol problems can go undetected allowing the problem with alcohol to continue.

The elderly are also susceptible to abusing alcohol, and the alcohol problems that can result, for a number of reasons including: loss of a loved one, social upheaval, retirement, a move to a retirement or nursing home, the onset of an illness to oneself or a loved one.

Studies have shown that alcohol-related medical problems put the elderly into the hospital as frequently as heart attacks. There is also an increased risk for falls and other accidents in the elderly who abuse alcohol.

Most elderly people are taking at least one prescription drug a day putting them at increased risk for negative alcohol-medication interactions. The elderly need to be made aware of how their particular prescription drug interacts with alcohol. Even small amounts of alcohol can have negative health effects with a host of commonly prescribed drugs and undermine their effectiveness. Any alcohol-medication interaction that has a sedative effect can be particularly dangerous leading to falls and other accidents.

Due to the difficulty in determining whether an elderly person is abusing alcohol, it is imperative that health care providers discuss alcohol use with their older patients as part of routine care. The elderly generally respond well to treatment for their alcohol problems particularly those who took up drinking later in life. The elderly deserve the same opportunity as the rest of the population to get the treatment they need.

What are some facts about drinking and driving?

Drinking and driving is a deadly combination with drunk driving being the most frequently committed violent crime in the United States. Each year, approximately 17,000 people die in alcohol-related traffic accidents, nearly one million people are injured and thousands are permanently disabled.

A drunk driver can be anyone - a social drinker, an occasional drinker as well as a chronic alcohol abuser or alcoholic. A drunk driver can kill or injure innocent people - pedestrians, motorcyclists, bicyclists, people standing or children playing near a street, passengers in the drunk driver's car or the occupants of the vehicle he or she hits. Children, playing in their own front yards, have been killed by drunk drivers!

Alcohol affects driving skills by impairing reaction time, reflexes and coordination. Alcohol also impairs vision, perception and judgment. The impairment process begins with the first drink and most people are severely impaired before they become legally intoxicated. A driver is legally intoxicated when his or her blood alcohol content (BAC) reaches the legal limit, either .10 or .08 for adults and .00 or .02 for those under 21, depending in which state you are.

If you do not drink and find yourself in a social situation where your ride home from the social function has had too much to drink, do not take a chance: find another ride, offer to drive the drinker home or call a taxi. Riding with a driver who has been drinking is just as dangerous as driving while drinking.

You do not need to have a problem with drinking, however, to be a drunk driver. Just one drink too many in a celebratory situation can put you at risk for a costly accident or a DUI (driving under the influence) conviction and the possibility of having yourself or another killed or injured. The rule - do not drive when you have been drinking, and do not ride with anyone who has been drinking - is the only one to live by. Lives are at risk.

A study in California showed that the real life, out-of-pocket costs for a first time DUI is close to $11,000 which includes fines, penalties, towing, alcohol education classes, auto insurance premium increases, drivers license reissuance and legal fees. The $11,000 amount assumes no injury, property damage or lost lives. This statistic makes the "Don't Drink and Drive" message take on a whole new meaning.

Studies show that two out of five Americans will be involved in an alcohol-related crash during their lifetime. This statistic underscores the need to help alcoholics to treatment and get them off the road as drunk drivers.

The "drunk driver" term also applies to people who bicycle, motorcycle, operate a boat, other watercraft or snowmobile while intoxicated. It is not just drunk drivers of cars and trucks who are hazardous and put lives at risk.

Knowing is not enough; we must apply.
Willing is not enough; we must do.

Goethe

CHAPTER 11

Where to Find Help

To find the help you need, contact one of the organizations or agencies listed below. Be cautious when selecting a facility or program. Ask questions; ask for referrals. Remember to keep looking until you find the facility or program best suited to your needs.

The listings are divided into three sections:

NATIONAL RESOURCES

These valuable resources include organizations that will provide you with general information, referral information for treatment facilities in all states, literature on alcohol abuse and alcoholism, and support group information.

STATE AUTHORITIES

Your state authority can refer you to a program, agency, organization or hospital that deals with alcohol abuse and alcoholism.

WHERE TO FIND HELP STATE BY STATE

You will find a selection of organizations, agencies and treatment facilities in towns and cities in your state. The listings have been selected for the following reasons and do not imply an endorsement by the author and/or publisher: offer either detoxification, referral, prevention, treatment or have a hotline, preferably with a toll-free number. If you would like a more comprehensive listing of where to find help in a particular state, contact the state authority or one of the national referral agencies.

NATIONAL RESOURCES

Al-Anon Family Group
1600 Corporate Landing Parkway
Virginia Beach, VA 23454
(800) 356-9996
www.al-anon.alateen.org

Alcohol Treatment Referrals
Substance Abuse Mental Health Services Administration
(800) 662-HELP
www.health.org/phone.htm#phone

Alcoholics Anonymous
PO Box 459, Grand Central Station
New York, NY 10163
(212) 870-3400
www.alcoholics-anonymous.org

MADD National Headquarters
PO Box 541688
Dallas, TX 75354-1688
(800) GET-MADD
www.madd.org

National Clearinghouse for Alcohol & Drug Information
PO Box 2345
Rockville, MD 20847
(800) 729-6686
www.health.org

National Council on Alcoholism & Drug Dependence
12 West 21st Street
New York, NY 10010
(800) NCA-CALL
(212) 206-6770
www.ncadd.org

National Institute on Alcohol Abuse & Alcoholism
6000 Executive Blvd.
Bethesda, MD 20892
(301) 443-3860
www.niaaa.nih.gov

Rational Recovery
PO Box 800
Lotus, CA 95651
(916) 621-2667
(800) 303-2873

Secular Organizations for Sobriety (SOS)
5521 Grosvenor Blvd.
Los Angeles, LA 90066
(301) 821-8430

Women for Sobriety
PO Box 618
Quakertown, PA 18951
(800) 333-1606
www.mediapulse.com/wfs

STATE AUTHORITIES

Alabama
Substance Abuse Services
PO Box 301410
Montgomery, AL 36130
(334) 242-3952

Alaska
Division of Alcoholism & Drug Abuse
PO Box 11607
Juneau, AK 99811
(907) 465-2071

Arizona
Bureau of Substance Abuse Services
2122 East Highland
Phoenix, AZ 85016
(602) 553-9092

Arkansas
Bureau of Alcohol & Drug Abuse
Prevention
5800 West 10th Street
Little Rock, AR 72204
(501) 280-4501

California
Governor's Policy Council on Drug &
Alcohol Abuse
1700 K Street, 5th Floor
Sacramento, CA 95814
(916) 445-1943

Colorado
Alcohol & Drug Abuse Division
4055 South Lowell Blvd.
Denver, CO 80236
(303) 866-7486

Connecticut
Dept. of Mental Health & Addiction
Services
410 Capitol Avenue
Hartford, CT 06134
(860) 418-6959

Delaware
Alcohol & Drug Services
1901 North DuPont Highway
Newcastle, DE 19720
(302) 577-4465

District of Columbia
Alcohol & Drug Abuse Services
Administration
1300 First Street, NE.
Washington, DC 20002
(202) 645-5556

Florida
Department of Children & Families
1317 Winewood Blvd.
Tallahassee, FL 32399
(904) 487-2920

Georgia
Division of Mental Health
2 Peachtree Street, NE
Atlanta, GA 30303
(404) 657-2273

Hawaii
Alcohol & Drug Abuse Division
1270 Queen Emma Street
Honolulu, HI 96813
(808) 586-3962

Idaho
Bureau of Mental Health & Substance
Abuse
PO Box 83720
Boise, ID 83720
(208) 334-6680

Illinois
Dept. of Alcoholism & Substance Abuse
100 West Randolph
Chicago, IL 60601
(312) 814-2291

Indiana
Family & Social Services Administration
402 West Washington Street
Indianapolis, IN 46204
(317) 232-7845

Iowa
Division of Substance Abuse & Health
Promotion
Lucas State Office Building
Des Moines, IA 50319
(515) 281-4417

Kansas
Alcohol & Drug Abuse Services
610 SW 10th Street
Topeka, KS 66612
(785) 296-3925

Kentucky
Division of Substance Abuse
100 Fair Oaks
Frankfort, KY 40621
(502) 564-2880

Louisiana
Office of Alcohol & Drug Abuse
1201 Capitol Access Road
Baton Rouge, LA 70821
(504) 342-6717

Maine
Office of Substance Abuse
159 State House Station
Augusta, ME 04333
(207) 287-6342

Maryland
Alcohol & Drug Abuse Administration
201 West Preston Street
Baltimore, MD 21201
(410) 767-6925

Massachusetts
Bureau of Substance Abuse Services
250 Washington Street
Boston, MA 02108
(617) 624-5151

Michigan
Bureau of Substance Abuse Services
320 South Walnut Street
Lansing, MI 48913
(517) 335-0278

Minnesota
Chemical Dependency Program Division
444 Lafayette Road
St. Paul, MN 55155
(612) 296-4728

Mississippi
Division of Alcohol & Drug Abuse
239 North Lamar Street
Jackson, MS 39201
(601) 359-1288

Missouri
Division of Alcohol & Drug Abuse
1706 East Elm Street
Jefferson City, MO 65101
(573) 751-7814

Montana
Addictive & Mental Disorders Division
1400 Broadway
Helena, MT 59620
(406) 444-3969

Nebraska
Division of Alcoholism, Drug Abuse &
Addiction Services
PO Box 94728
Lincoln, NE 68509
(402) 471-2851

Nevada
Bureau of Alcohol & Drug Abuse
505 East King Street
Carson City, NV 89710
(702) 687-4790

New Hampshire
Bureau of Substance Abuse Services
105 Pleasant Street
Concord, NH 03301
(603) 271-6105

New Jersey
Division of Alcoholism, Drug Abuse &
Addiction
120 South Stockton Street
Trenton, NJ 08625
(609) 292-9068

New Mexico
Behavioral Health Services Division
1190 St. Francis Drive
Sante Fe, NM 87501
(505) 827-0578

New York
Office of Alcoholism & Substance Abuse
Services
1450 Western Avenue
Albany, NY 12203
(518) 457-2061

North Carolina
Substance Abuse Services
325 North Salisbury Street
Raleigh, NC 27603
(919) 733-46670

North Dakota
Division of Mental Health & Substance
Abuse Services
600 South 2nd Street
Bismarck, ND 58504
(701) 328-8922

Ohio
Dept. of Alcohol & Drug Addiction
Services
280 North High Street
Columbus, OH 43215
(614) 466-3445

Oklahoma
Dept. of Mental Health & Substance
Abuse Services
1200 Northeast 13, 2nd Floor
Oklahoma City, OK 73117
(405) 522-3650

Oregon
Office of Alcohol & Drug Abuse
500 Summer Street, NE
Salem, OR 97310
(503) 945-5763

Pennsylvania
Bureau of Alcohol & Drug Programs
2635 Praxton Street
Harrisburg, PA 17111
(717) 783-8200

Rhode Island
Division of Substance Abuse
3 Capitol Hill
Providence, RI 02908
(401) 277-4680

South Carolina
Dept. of Alcohol & Other Drug Abuse
Services
3700 Forest Drive
Columbia, SC 29204
(803) 734-9520

South Dakota
Division of Alcohol & Drug Abuse
Hillsview Plaza
East Highway 34
Pierre, SD 57501
(605) 773-3123

Tennessee
Bureau of Alcohol & Other Drug Abuse
Services
425 5th Avenue, North
Nashville, TN 37219
(615) 741-1921

Texas
Commission on Alcohol & Drug Abuse
9001 North IH 35
Austin, TX 78753
(512) 349-6601
(800) 832-9623

Utah
Division of Substance Abuse
120 North 200 West
Salt Lake City, UT 84103
(801) 538-3939

Vermont
Office of Alcohol & Drug Abuse Programs
108 Cherry Street
Burlington, VT 05402
(802) 651-1550

Virginia
Office of Substance Abuse Services
109 Governor Street
Richmond, VA 23219
(804) 786-3906

Washington
Division of Alcohol & Substance Abuse
612 Woodland Square Loop, SE
Olympia, WA 98504
(360) 438-8200

West Virginia
Division of Alcoholism & Drug Abuse
1900 Kanawha Blvd.
Charleston, WV 25305
(304) 558-2276

Wisconsin
Bureau of Substance Abuse Services
1 West Wilson Street
Madison, WI 53707
(608) 266-3719

Wyoming
Division of Behavioral Health
2300 Capitol Avenue
Cheyenne, WY 82002
(307) 777-6494

WHERE TO FIND HELP STATE BY STATE

ALABAMA

Anniston
Calhoun Mental Health Center
331 East 8th Street
Anniston, AL 36202
(256) 236-3403

Birmingham
Alcoholism Recovery Services
2701 Jefferson Avenue SW
Birmingham, AL 35211
(205) 923-6552

Family & Child Services
5201 Airport Highway
Birmingham, AL 35212
(205) 510-2600

University of Alabama
UAB Substance Abuse Programs
401 Beacon Parkway West
Birmingham, AL 35209
(205) 917-3784

Calera
Chilton Shelby Mental Health Center
182 17th Street
Calera, AL 35045
(205) 668-2700

Centre
Cherokee County Alcoholism/Substance
Abuse Council
Cherokee County Courthouse Annex
Centre, AL 35960
(256) 927-3111

Decatur
Mental Health Center of North Central AL
1312 Somerville Road
Decatur, AL 35601
(256) 353-9116

Demopolis
West Alabama Mental Health Center
1215 South Walnut Avenue
Demopolis, AL 36732
(334) 289-2410
Hotline: (800) 239-2901

Dothan
Spectra Care
831 John D. Odom Road
Dothan, AL 36303
(334) 794-3771
Hotline: (334) 794-0300

Guntersville
Marshall/Jackson MH Authority
22165 Highway 431
Guntersville, AL 35976
(256) 582-4465

Huntsville
Columbia Medical Center of Huntsville
One Hospital Drive
Huntsville, AL 35801
(256) 880-4260
Hotline: (256) 880-4280

Jasper
Northwest Alabama Mental Health Center
1100 7th Avenue
Jasper, AL 35501
(205) 387-0541
Hotline: (800) 489-3971

Montgomery
Chemical Addictions Program Inc.
1153 Air Base Blvd.
Montgomery, AL 36108
(334) 265-4544

Council on Substance Abuse
100 Commerce Street
Montgomery, AL 36104
(334) 262-1629

Opelika
East Alabama MH/MR Center
2506 Hamilton Road
Opelika, AL 36801
(334) 742-2700
Hotline: (800) 815-0630

Rogersville
Substance Abuse Council of NW AL Inc.
Route 4
Rogersville, AL 35652
(256) 247-1222

Russellville
Sunrise Lodge
1163 Washington Avenue SW
Russellville, AL 35653
(256) 332-0078

Spanish Fort
The Shoulder
4901 Battleship Parkway
Spanish Fort, AL 36577
(334) 626-2199

Troy
East Central Mental Health
200 Cherry Street
Troy, AL 36081
(334) 566-6022

Tuscaloosa
Indian Rivers Mental Health Center
505 19th Avenue
Tuscaloosa, AL 35401
(205) 391-0118

Wetumpka
Bradford Health Services
500 Hospital Drive
Wetumpka, AL 36092
(256) 567-4311

ALASKA

Anchorage
Alaska Human Services Inc.
4050 Lake Otis Parkway
Anchorage, AK 99508
(907) 561-4535

Charter North Star
2530 Debarr Road
Anchorage, AK 99508
(907) 258-7575
Hotline: (800) 478-7575

Salvation Army
1709 South Bragaw Street
Anchorage, AK 99508
(907) 276-2898

Volunteers of America
441 West 5th Avenue
Anchorage, AK 99501
(907) 279-9634

Barrow
North Slope Borough
Health Substance Abuse Treatment
Services
579 Kingosak Street
Barrow, AK 99723
(907) 852-0274

Cordova
Cordova Community Medical Center
602 Chase Avenue
Cordova, AK 99574
(907) 424-8300

Fairbanks
Regional Center for Alcohol & Other
Addictions
3100 South Cushman Street
Fairbanks, AK 99707
(907) 452-6251

Tanana Chiefs Conference Inc.
122 1st Avenue
Fairbanks, AK 99701
(907) 366-7269

Juneau
National Council on Alcoholism & Drug
Dependence
211 4th Street
Juneau, AK 99801
(907) 463-3755
Hotline: (800) 654-4073

Ketchikan
Gateway Center for Human Services
3050 5th Avenue
Ketchikan, AK 99901
(907) 225-4154

Kodiak
Kodiak Council on Alcoholism Inc.
115 Mill Bay Road
Kodiak, AK 99615
(907) 486-3535

Nome
Northern Lights Recovery Center
5th Avenue & Division Streets
Nome, AK 99762
(907) 443-3344
Hotline: (800) 898-5463

ARIZONA

Chandler
Chandler Valley Hope & Drug Treatment
Center
501 North Washington Street
Chandler, AZ 85225
(602) 899-3335

Flagstaff
Aspen Hill Behavioral Health Systems
305 West Forest Avenue
Flagstaff, AZ 86001
(520) 773-1060
Hotline: (800) 336-2773

Kingman
Mohave Mental Health Clinic
1750 Beverly Street
Kingman, AZ 86401
(520) 757-8111

Mesa
East Valley Addiction Council Inc.
554 South Bellview Street
Mesa, AZ 85204
(602) 962-7922

Parker
Indian Hospital Substance Abuse Services
Route 1
Parker, AZ 85344
(520) 669-2137

Phoenix
National Council on Alcoholism & Drug
Dependency
2701 North 16th Street
Phoenix, AZ 85006
(602) 264-6214
Hotline: (602) 285-1064

Saint Lukes Behavioral Health Center
1800 East Van Buren Street
Phoenix, AZ 85006
(602) 251-8484
Hotline: (602) 251-8535

Treatment Assessment Screening Center
2234 North 7th Street
Phoenix, AZ 85006
(602) 254-7328
Hotline: 222-9444

Prescott
West Yavapai Guidance Clinic
505 South Cortez Street
Prescott, AZ 86301
(520) 445-7730

Tucson
Cottonwood de Tucson
4110 West Sweetwater Drive
Tucson, AZ 85745-9348
(520) 743-0411

Sierra Tucson Inc.
16500 North Lago del Oro Parkway
Tucson, AZ 85739
(520) 624-4000

Tucson Council on Alcoholism & Drug
Dependence
1230 East Broadway
Tucson, AZ 85719
(602) 620-6615

ARKANSAS

Fort Smith
Gateway House
3900 North Armour Avenue
Fort Smith, AR 72904-4317
(501) 783-8849
Hotline: (800) 886-4600

Western Arkansas Counseling & Guidance
Center
3113 South 70th Street
Fort Smith, AR 72903
(501) 478-6664

Gassville
OMART inc.
16 Snowball Drive
Gassville, AR 72635
(870) 435-6200

Jonesboro
Greenleaf Center Inc.
2712 East Johnson Avenue
Jonesboro, AR 72401
(501) 932-2800
Hotline: (800) 800-0496

Little Rock
Baptist Rehabilitation Institute
9601 Interstate 630
Little Rock, AR 72205
(501) 202-7507

CPC Pinnacle Pointe Hospital
11501 Financial Center Parkway
Little Rock, AR 72211
(501) 223-3322

Mid Arkansas Substance Abuse Services
4601 West 7th Street
Little Rock, AR 72205
(501) 686-9393

North Little Rock
Family Service Agency of Central Arkansas
628 West Broadway
North Little Rock, AR 72114
(501) 373-4242

Pine Bluff
Southeast Arkansas Behavioral Healthcare Inc.
2500 Rike Drive
Pine Bluff, AR 71613
(870) 534-1834

Springdale
Decision Point Inc.
301 Holcomb Street
Springdale, AR 72765
(501) 756-1060

CALIFORNIA

Auburn
Sierra Council on Alcohol & Drug
Dependency
610 Auburn Ravine Road
Auburn, CA 95603
(916) 885-1961

Bakersfield
Alta Vista
5201 White Lane
Bakersfield, CA 93309
(805) 398-1800

Berkeley
Berkeley Addiction Treatment Services
2975 Sacramento Street
Berkeley, CA 94702
(510) 644-0200

Blythe
Riverside County Substance Abuse Program
1267 West Hobson Way
Blythe, CA 92225
(619) 921-7870

Carson
Kaiser Permanente
23621 South Main Street
Carson, CA 90745
(310) 513-6707

Chico
Butte County Dept. of Behavioral Health
564 Rio Lindo Avenue
Chico, CA 95926
(530) 895-6617
Hotline: (800) 371-4373

Clearlake
Alcohol & Other Drug Services
7000 B South Center Drive
Clearlake, CA 95422
(707) 994-7617
Hotline: (707) 263-8552

Concord
Mount Diablo Medical Pavilion
2740 Grant Street
Concord, CA 94520
(510) 674-4160

Recovery Management Services
2885 Concord Blvd.
Concord, CA 94519
(510) 682-5704

Costa Mesa
Newport Mesa Alcohol & Drug House
3115 Redhill Avenue
Costa Mesa, CA 92626
(714) 850-8431

Deer Park
St. Helena Hospital Alcohol Center
650 Sanitarium Road
Deer Park, CA 94576
(800) 454-4673

El Centro
Volunteers of America
1331-B Clark Road
El Centro, CA 92243
(619) 353-8482

El Monte
Mid Valley Recovery Services
3430 Cogswell Road
El Monte, CA 91732
(626) 453-3460

Eureka
Alcohol Drug Care Service Inc.
135 C Street
Eureka, CA 95501
(707) 445-3869

Fontana
Merrill Community Services
16846 Merrill Avenue
Fontana, CA 92335
(909) 823-0609

Fresno
Alcoholism & Drug Abuse Council
4411 North Cedar Avenue
Fresno, CA 93726
(209) 248-1548

Glendale
Alpha Recovery Center
1330 South Glendale Avenue
Glendale, CA 91205
(818) 502-2300

Hanford
Alcohol/Drug Education & Counseling
Center
1393 Bailey Drive
Hanford, CA 93230
(209) 582-4481

Hayward
Hayward Community Center
22297 Mission Blvd.
Hayward, CA 94541
(510) 886-8696

Inglewood
El Dorado Community Service Center
4450 West Century Blvd.
Inglewood, CA 90304
(310) 671-055

Lakewood
Lakewood Regional Medical Center
3700 East South Street
Lakewood, CA 90712
(800) 451-1131

Long Beach
Alcohol Education & Recovery Center
1355 Redondo Avenue
Long Beach, CA 90804
(562) 986-5046

Long Beach Alcohol & Drug Rehab Program
2525 Grand Avenue
Long Beach, CA 90815
(310) 570-4100

Los Angeles
Bay Area Addiction Research &
Treatment
1020 West Olympic Blvd.
Los Angeles, CA 90015
(213) 747-2267

Dial Alcohol & Drug Education Center
3540 Wilshire Blvd.
Los Angeles, CA 90010
(213) 384-5353

East Los Angeles Alcoholism Council
916 South Atlantic Blvd.
Los Angeles, CA 90022
(213) 268-9344

National Council on Alcoholism & Drug
Dependency
3325 Wilshire Blvd.
Los Angeles, CA 90010
(213) 384-0403

Madera
Madera Counseling Center
14277 Road 28
Madera, CA 93638
(209) 673-3508

Modesto
Stanislaus County Substance Abuse Services
1501 F Street
Modesto, CA 95354
(209) 558-7466

North Hollywood
Dial Alcohol & Drug Education Center
12034 Vanowen Street
North Hollywood, CA 91605
(818) 765-1232

Oakland
John George Family Recovery Center
3229 Elm Street
Oakland, CA 94609
(510) 596-4189
Hotline: (510) 450-0881

Merritt Peralta Institute
3012 Summit Street
Oakland, CA 94609
(510) 869-8850

West Oakland Health Council
3007 Telegraph Avenue
Oakland, CA 94609
(510) 433-1500

Oxnard
Ventura County Dept. of Behavioral
Health
2651 South C Street
Oxnard, CA 93033
(805) 385-1885

Palo Alto
North County Alcohol Services Center
231 Grant Avenue
Palo Alto, CA 94306
(650) 328-1441
Hotline: (800) 488-9919

Pasadena
Pasadena Council on Alcoholism & Drug
Dependency
Referral Agency
181 North Hudson Avenue
Pasadena, CA 91101
(818) 795-9127

Placerville
El Dorado Council on Alcoholism
2810 Coloma Road
Placerville, CA 95667
(530) 622-8193

Pleasant Hill
Alcohol & Drug Abuse Council of Conta
Costa Inc.
171 Mayhew Way
Pleasant Hill, CA 94523
(510) 932-8100

Pomona
National Council on Alcohol & Drug
Dependency
375 South Main Street
Pomona, CA 91766
(909) 629-4084

Rancho Mirage
Betty Ford Center at Eisenhower
3900 Bob Hope Drive
Rancho Mirage, CA 92270
(760) 773-4100
Hotline: (800) 854-9211

Riverside
Riverside County Substance Abuse
Program
1777 Atlanta Avenue
Riverside CA 92507
(909) 275-2125
Hotline: (800) 499-3008

Sacramento
Gateway Recovery House
4049 Miller Way
Sacramento, CA 95817
(916) 451-9312

The Effort Counseling Center
1820 J Street
Sacramento, CA 95816
(916) 444-6296

Salinas
Community Human Services
1101 F North Main Street
Salinas, CA 93906
(408) 424-4828

San Bernadino
San Bernadino County Office of Alcohol
& Drug Treatment Services
565 North Mount Vernon Drive
San Bernadino, CA 92411
(909) 387-7677
Hotline: (800) 331-3237

San Diego
Kaiser Permanente Medical Group
3420 Kenyon Street
San Diego, CA 92110
(619) 221-6550

Mental Health Systems
6153 Fairmount Avenue
San Diego, CA 92120
(619) 281-1292
Hotline: (800) 479-3339

Scripps Clinic
4320 La Jolla Village Drive
San Diego, CA 92122
(619) 622-0394

Volunteers of America
1111 Island Avenue
San Diego, CA 92101
(619) 232-5171

San Francisco
Freedom From Alcohol & Drugs
1353 48th Avenue
San Francisco, CA 94122
(415) 665-8077

Haight Ashbury Free Clinics
766 Stanyan Street
San Francisco, CA 94117
(415) 487-5622

National Council on Alcohol & Drug
Abuse
944 Market Street
San Francisco, CA 94102
(415) 296-9900

Salvation Army Harborlight Center
1275 Harrison Street
San Francisco, CA 94103
(415) 864-7000

San Jose
Alum Rock Counseling Center
1245 East Santa Clara Street
San Jose, CA 95116
(408) 294-0500

Central Treatment & Recovery Center
976 Lenzen Avenue
San Jose, CA 95126
(408) 299-7280
Hotline: (800) 488-9919

San Leandro
Horizon Community Center
1403 164th Avenue
San Leandro, CA 94578
(510) 278-8654

San Mateo
Horizon Services
2251 Palm Avenue
San Mateo, CA 94403
(650) 345-8265

San Pedro
Peninsula Recovery Center
1386 West 7th Street
San Pedro, CA 90732
(310) 513-5300

San Rafael
Marin Treatment Center
1466 Lincoln Avenue
San Rafael, CA 94901
(415) 457-3755

Santa Ana
Santa Ana Alcohol & Drug Abuse Services
1200 North Main Street
Santa Ana, CA 92701
(714) 568-4165

Santa Barbara
Council on Alcoholism & Drug Abuse
232 East Canon Perdido Street
Santa Barbara, CA 93102
(805) 963-1433

Santa Monica
Alcoholism Council West Area
1424 4th Street
Santa Monica, CA 90401
(310) 451-5881

Santa Rosa
Sonoma County Alcohol & Drug Abuse
Services
2759 Bennett Valley Road
Santa Rosa, CA 95404
(707) 524-7450

South Lake Tahoe
Sierra Recovery Services
2677 Reaves Street
South Lake Tahoe, CA 96150
(916) 541-5440

Stockton
San Joaquin County Chemical
Dependency Counseling Center
620 North Aurora Street
Stockton, CA 95202
(209) 468-3720

Susanville
Lassen County Alcohol & Drug program
476 Alexander Avenue
Susanville, CA 96130
(530) 251-8112

Torrance
National Council on Alcohol & Drug
Dependency
1334 Post Avenue
Torrance, CA 90501
(310) 328-1460

Ukiah
Mendocino County Public Health Dept.
302 West Henry Street
Ukiah, CA 95482
(707) 463-5672

Van Nuys
National Council on Alcoholism and Drug
Dependency
14557 Friar Street
Van Nuys, CA 91411
(818) 997-0414

Visalia
Alcohol & Drug Services of Tulare County
2223 North Shirk Road
Visalia, CA 93291
(209) 651-8090

Walnut Creek
Walnut Creek Hospital
175 La Casa Via
Walnut Creek, CA 94598
(925) 933-7990
Hotline: (888) 800-4968

Watsonville
Santa Cruz Community Counseling Center
161 Miles Lane
Watsonville, CA 95076
(408) 761-5667

COLORADO

Aurora
Lifecare Foundation
1290 South Potomac Street
Aurora, CO 80012
(303) 745-2273
Hotline: (800) 458-2273

Boulder
Boulder County Health Dept. Recovery
Systems
3450 Broadway
Boulder, CO 80304
(303) 441-1138

Canon City
Rocky Mountain Behavioral Health Inc.
618 Main Street
Canon City, CO 81215
(719) 275-7650

Colorado Springs
El Paso County Dept. of Health
301 South Union Blvd.
Colorado Springs, CO 80910
(719) 578-3150
Hotline: (888) 845-2881

Delta
Options Counseling Center
261 Hartig Drive
Delta, CO 81416
(303) 874-0535

Denver
Alcohol Counseling Services of CO Inc.
1300 South Lafayette Drive
Denver, CO 80210
(303) 777-8648

Community Alcohol/Drug Rehab &
Education Center
3315 Gilpin Street
Denver, CO 80205
(303) 295-2521

Mile High Council on Alcohol Drug Abuse
1444 Wazee Street
Denver, CO 80202
(303) 825-8113

Salvation Army Adult Rehab Center
4751 Broadway
Denver, CO 80216
(303) 293-3441

Estes Park
Harmony Foundation Inc.
1600 Fish Hatchery Road
Estes Park, CO 80517
(970) 586-4491

Fort Collins
Seven Lakes Recovery Program
2362 East Prospect Avenue
Fort Collins, CO 80525
(970) 484-0121

Grand Junction
Dos Rios Counseling Service
1008 North 5th Street
Grand Junction, CO 81501
(970) 241-3091

Lakewood
Jefferson County Health Dept. Substance
Abuse Counseling Program
260 South Kipling Street
Lakewood, CO 80226
(303) 239-7162

Littleton
Southwest Counseling Associates
141 West Davies Avenue
Littleton, CO 80120
(303) 730-1717

Pueblo
CO Mental Health Institute
1600 West 24th Street
Pueblo, CO 81003
(719) 546-4797

CONNECTICUT

Bloomfield
Blue Ridge Center
1095 Blue Hills Avenue
Bloomfield, CT 06002
(860) 243-1331

Bridgeport
Guenster Rehabilitation Services Inc.
276 Union Avenue
Bridgeport, CT 06607
(203) 384-9301
Hotline: (888) 822-2270

Bridgewater
Midwestern CT Council on Alcoholism
132 Hut Hill Road
Bridgewater, CT 06752
(860) 354-4423

Hartford
Alcohol & Drug Recovery Centers Inc.
500 Vine Street
Hartford, CT 06112
(860) 769-6680

Community Health Services Inc.
520 Albany Avenue
Hartford, CT 06120
(860) 249-9625

Middletown
Rushford Center Inc.
1250 Silver Street
Middletown, CT 06457
(860) 346-0300

New Haven
Affiliates for Consultation & Therapy
389 Orange Street
New Haven, CT 06511
(203) 562-4235

Connecticut Mental Health Center
1 Long Wharf Drive
New Haven, CT 06511
(203) 789-7817

New London
SE Council on Alcohol & Drug
Dependency
100 Bank Street
New London, CT 06320
(860) 889-1717

Norwalk
Connecticut Counseling Centers
20 North Main Street
Norwalk, CT 06854
(203) 838-6508
Hotline: (800) 203-1234

Norwich
SE Council on Alcohol & Drug
Dependency
313 Main Street
Norwich, CT 06360
(860) 889-3414

Sandy Hook
Cornerstone of Eagle Hill
32 Albert Hills Road
Sandy Hook, CT 06482
(203) 426-8085
Hotline: (800) 334-4744

Stamford
Liberation & Meridian Programs
119 Main Street
Stamford, CT 06901
(203) 359-3134

Waterbury
Family Service of Greater Waterbury
34 Murray Street
Waterbury, CT 06710
(203) 756-8317

Center for Alcohol/Drug Free Living
26 North Elm Street
Waterbury, CT 06702
(860) 755-1143
Hotline: (203) 574-1419

DELAWARE

Dover
Phoenix Mental Health Services
567 South Governors Avenue
Dover, DE 19904
(302) 736-6135

Georgetown
Children & Family Trust
410 South Bedford Street
Georgetown, DE 1994-1850
(302) 856-2388

Wilmington
Counseling & Recovery Services Inc.
114 Senatorial Drive
Wilmington, DE 19807
(302) 658-1888

Family & Children Services
2005 Baynard Blvd.
Wilmington, DE 19802
(302) 658-5177

Peoples Settlement Association
408 East 8th Street
Wilmington, DE 19801
(302) 658-4133

DISTRICT OF COLUMBIA

Washington
Addiction Prevention & Recovery Administration
1900 Massachusetts Avenue
Washington, DC 20003
(202) 727-5163

Concerned Citizens on Alcohol & Drug Abuse Inc.
3115 Martin Luther King Jr. Avenue SE
Washington, DC 20032
(202) 563-3210

Georgetown Medical Center
3800 Reservoir Road NW
Washington, DC 20007
(202) 687-8770

Psychiatric Institute of Washington
4228 Wisconsin Avenue NW
Washington, DC 20016
(202) 965-8550

FLORIDA

Belle Glade
New Beginnings
149 SE Avenue D
Belle Glade, FL 33430
(561) 992-1686

Boca Raton
National Recovery Institute
1000 NW 15th Street
Boca Raton, FL 33486
(305) 792-2888
Hotline: (800) 762-0896

Bradenton
Manatee Glens Hospital
2020 26th Avenue East
Bradenton, FL 34208
(941) 741-3805
Hotline: (941) 741-3805

Clearwater
Family Services Center
2188 58th Street
Clearwater, FL 34620
(813) 539-0492

Daytona Beach
Adult Clinical Services Center
330 North Street
Daytona Beach, FL 32114
(904) 255-0447
Hotline: (904) 9471300

Milestones Inc.
1501 Ridgewood Drive
Daytona Beach, FL 32117
(904) 673-6227

Delray Beach
Drug Abuse Foundation of Palm Beach County
400 South Swinton Avenue
Delray Beach, FL 33444
(561) 278-0000

Fort Lauderdale
American Family Centers Inc.
6250 North Andrews Avenue
Fort Lauderdale, FL 33309
(954) 772-9842

Broward Addiction Recovery Center
601 South Andrews Avenue
Fort Lauderdale, FL 33301
(954) 765-5105

Fort Myers
SW FL Addiction Services Inc.
2101 McGregor Blvd.
Fort Myers, FL 33901
(941) 332-6937

Fort Pierce
Drug Abuse Treatment Association Inc.
4590 Selvitz Road
Fort Pierce, FL 34981
(561) 464-7540
Hotline: (800) 253-8770

Gainesville
Meridian Behavioral Healthcare Inc.
4300 SW 13th Street
Gainesville, FL 32608
(352) 374-5600

Hialeah
Dade Family Counseling Inc.
1490 West 49th Place
Hialeah, FL 33012
(305) 827-3252

Hollywood
Broward Addiction Recovery Center
6491 Taft Street
Hollywood, FL 33024
(954) 964-0515

Jacksonville
Gateway Community Services Inc.
555 Stockton Street
Jacksonville, FL 32204

River Region Human Services Inc.
660 Park Street
Jacksonville, FL 32204
(904) 359-2680

Key West
Lower Florida Keys Health Systems Inc.
1200 Kennedy Drive
Key West, FL 33040
(305) 294-5535

Miami
Community Health of South Dade Inc.
10300 SW 216th Street
Miami, FL 33190
(305) 252-4840

Metro Dade Office of Rehab Services
11575 NW 7th Avenue
Miami, FL 33138
(305) 953-5125

Miami Behavioral Center
2140 West Flager Street
Miami, FL 33135
(305) 643-8012

Mount Sinai Medical Group
4300 Alton Road
Miami, FL 33140
(305) 674-2942

South Miami Hospital
7400 SW 62nd Avenue
Miami, FL 33143
(305) 662-8118
Holtline: (800) 937-4673

The Village South Inc.
4900 NE 2nd Avenue
Miami, FL 33137
(305) 573-3784
Hotline: (800) 443-3784

Naples
David Lawrence Center
6075 Golden Gate Parkway
Naples, FL 33999
(813) 649-1404

New Port Richey
Harbor Behavioral Health Care Institute
5390 School Road
New Port Richey, FL 34653
(813) 841-430

Ocala
Marion/Citrus Mental Health Center
717 SW Martin Luther King Jr. Avenue
Ocala, FL 34474
(352) 620-7361
Hotline: (352) 629-9595

Orlando
Center for Drug Free Living
100 West Columbia Street
Orlando, FL 32806
(407) 245-2500

Colonial Counseling Associates
9318 East Colonial Drive
Orlando, FL 32817
(407) 249-1146

Human Services Associates
1703 West Colonial Drive
Orlando, FL 32805
(407) 422-0880

Panama City
Chemical Addictions Recovery Effort
4000 East 3rd Street
Panama City, FL 32404
(904) 872-7676

Pensacola
Lakeview Center Inc.
1221 West Lakeview Avenue
Pensacola, FL 32501
(850) 438-1617

Saint Petersburg
Operation Par Inc.
10901-C Roosevelt Blvd.
Saint Petersburg, FL 33716
(813) 570-5080

Sanford
Grove Counseling Center
1501 East 8th Street
Sanford, FL 32771
(407) 339-9600
Hotline: (888) 532-4006

Sarasota
First Step of Sarasota
426 Central Avenue
Sarasota, FL 34236
(941) 362-3093

Tallahassee
Addiction Recovery Center
1835 Buford Court
Tallahassee, FL 32308
(850) 656-5112

Tampa
Agency for Community Treatment Services
4612 North 56th Street
Tampa, FL 33610
(813) 238-9505

Drug Abuse Comp. Coord. Office
3630 North 50th Street
Tampa, FL 33619
(813) 875-8116

West Palm Beach
Comp Alcoholism Rehab Programs
5400 East Avenue
West Palm Beach, FL 33402-2507
(561) 844-6400

Drug Abuse Treatment Association
1720 East Tiffany Drive
West Palm Beach, FL 33407
(561) 844-35567
Hotline: (800) 253-8700

GEORGIA

Atlanta
Charter Anchor Behavioral Health System
5454 Yorktowne Drive
Atlanta, GA 30349
(404) 991-6044
Hotline: (800) 252-6465

Fulton County Drug & Alcohol Treatment Center
265 Boulevard Street NE
Atlanta, GA 30312
(404) 730-1675

Augusta
CMHC of East Central Georgia
3421 Mike Padgett Hwy.
Augusta, GA 30906
(706) 771-4846
Hotline: (800) 766-6041

Columbus
St. Francis Hospital
Columbus, GA 31908
(706) 320-3700
Hotline: (800) 272-3236

Decatur
Clifton Springs Substance Abuse Services
3110 Clifton Springs Road
Decatur, GA 30034
(404) 244-4411

Dublin
Middle Georgia Alcohol & Drug Clinic
600 North Jefferson Street
Dublin, GA 31021
(912) 275-6800
Hotline: (912) 275-6810

Griffin
Substance Abuse Outpatient Services
of MacIntosh Trail MH Services
141 West Solomon Street
Griffin, GA 30223
(770) 229-3057
Hotline: (770) 358-5251

Macon
Charter Behavioral Health Systems of
Central Georgia
3500 Riverside Drive
Macon, GA 31210
(912) 474-6200
Hotline: (800) 242-7837

Saint Simons Island
Charter by the Seas
Behavioral Health Systems
2927 Demere Road
Saint Simons Island, GA 31522
(912) 638-1999
Hotline: (800) 821-7224

Smyrna
Ridgeview Institute
3995 South Cobb Drive
Smyrna, GA 30080
(770) 431-0005
Hotline: (800) 329-9775

HAWAII

Hilo
Drug Addiction Services of HI
305 Wailuku Drive
Hilo, HI 96720
(808) 961-6822

Honolulu
Coalition For A Drug Free Hawaii
1130 North Nimitz Highway
Honolulu, HI 96817
(808) 545-3228

Drug Addiction Services of HI
1130 North Nimitz Highway
Honolulu, HI 96817
(808) 538-0704

Salvation Army Addiction Treatment Services
3624 Waokanaka Street
Honolulu, HI 96817
(808) 595-6371

Kailua
Castle Medical Center
640 Ulukahiki Street
Kailua, HI 96734
(808) 263-5142
Hotline: (800) 224-1212

Lihue
Child & Family Service
4375 Puaole Street
Lihue, HI 96766
(808) 245-5914

Makawao
Aloha House Inc.
4593 Ike Drive
Makawao, HI 96768
(808) 579-9584

Wailuku
Maui Youth & Family Services
1650 Kaahumanu Avenue
Wailuku, HI 96793
(808) 984-5656

IDAHO

Boise
Alcoholism Intervention Services
8436 Fairview Avenue
Boise, ID 83704
(208) 322-8046

CPC Intermountain Hospital of Boise
303 North Allumbaugh Street
Boise, ID 83704
(208) 377-8400

Northview Hospital
8050 Northview Street
Boise, ID 83704
(208) 327-0504

Idaho Falls
Alcoholic Rehabilitation Association
163 East Elva Street
Idaho Falls, ID 83401
(208) 522-6012

Lewiston
Port of Hope Family Treatment Centers
828 8th Avenue
Lewiston, ID 83501
(208) 746-1442

Nampa
Port of Hope Centers Inc.
508 East Florida Street
Nampa, ID 83686
(208) 463-0118
Hotline: (800) 974-0118

ILLINOIS

Aurora
Community Counseling Center of Fox Valley
400 Mercy Lane
Aurora, IL 60506
(630) 897-0584

Bloomington
Chestnut Health Systems
1003 Martin Luther King Jr. Drive
Bloomington, IL 61701
(309) 827-6026

Champaign
Prairie Center Health Systems
122 West Hill Street
Champaign, IL 61820
(217) 356-7576
Hotline: (217) 328-4500

Chicago
City of Chicago - Interventions
140 North Ashland Avenue
Chicago, IL 60607
(312) 850-9411
Hotline: (800) 962-1126

Gateway Foundation Inc.
2615 West 63rd Street
Chicago, IL 60629
(773) 476-0622
Hotline: (800) 444-1331

Haymarket/Maryville Center
120 North Sangamon Street
Chicago, IL 60613
(312) 226-7984
Hotline: (312) 226-4357

Interventions
5701 South Wood Street
Chicago, IL 60636
(773) 737-4600
Hotline: (312) 737-8915

Mercy Hospital & Medical Center
2525 South Michigan Avenue
Chicago, IL 60616
(312) 567-2486

Parkside Recovery Center
2520 Lakeview Street
Chicago, IL 60614
(773) 388-6800

Southeast Alcohol & Drug Abuse Center
8640 South Chicago Avenue
Chicago, IL 60617
(773) 731-9100

Danville
Prairie Center Health Systems
200 West Williams Street
Danville, IL 61832
(217) 477-4500
Hotline: (217) 328-4500

Decatur
Decatur Mental Health Center
2300 North Edward Street
Decatur, IL 62526
(217) 362-6262

Des Plaines
Forest Clinic
555 Wilson Lane
Des Plaines, IL 60016
(847) 635-4100
Hotline: (800) 866-9600

Evanston
Peer Services Inc.
906 Davis Street
Evanston, IL 60201
(847) 492-1778

Hazel Crest
South Suburban Council on Alcoholism &
Substance Abuse
1909 Cheker Square
Hazel Crest, IL 60429
(708) 957-2854

Joliet
Saint Joseph Medical Center
333 North Madison Street
Joliet, IL 60435
(815) 741-7545

Kankakee
Riverside Resolve Center
401 North Wall Street
Kankakee, IL 60950
(815) 468-3241
Hotline: (800) 435-4635

Marion
Franklin/Williamson Human Services Inc.
1305 West Main Street
Marion, IL 62959
(618) 997-5336
Hotline: (800) 269-9981

Melrose Park
Westlake Community Hospital
1225 Lake Street
Melrose Park, IL 60160
(708) 938-7566

Peoria
Human Services Center
3500 West New Leaf Lane
Peoria, IL 61614
(309) 692-6900
Hotline: (309) 682-1119

Quincy
Great River Recovery Resource
428 South 36th Street
Quincy, IL 62301
(217) 224-6300

Rock Island
Robert Young Center for Community MH
2701 17th Street
Rock Island, IL 61201
(309) 793-2031

Rockford
PHASE Inc.
319 South Church Street
Rockford, IL 61101
(815) 962-0871
Hotline: (815) 962-6102

Salem
Community Resource Center
1325-C West Whitaker Street
Salem, IL 62881
(618) 533-1391

Skokie
Turning Point
8324 Skokie Blvd.
Skokie, IL 60077
(847) 933-0051

Springfield
Saint Johns Hospital
800 East Carpenter Street
Springfield, IL 62769
(217) 525-5629

Wheaton
DuPage County Health Dept.
1111 North County Farm Road
Wheaton, IL 60187
(630) 980-5364

Woodstock
Horizons Behavioral Health LLC
527 West South Street
Woodstock, IL 60098
(815) 338-9199

INDIANA

Anderson
Community Hospital of Anderson &
Madison County
1515 North Madison Avenue
Anderson, IN 46011
(765) 646-5120
Hotline: (765) 646-8066

Bloomington
Bloomington Meadows Hospital
3600 North Prow Road
Bloomington, IN 47404
(812) 331-8000

South Central Community MH Centers
221 North Rogers Street
Bloomington, IN 47401
(812) 339-1691

Columbus
Quinco Consulting Center
806 Jackson Street
Columbus, IN 47201
(812) 379-2341
Hotline: (800) 832-5472

Elkhart
Life Treatment Centers
130 South Taylor Street
Elkhart, IN 46601
(219) 233-5433
Hotline: (888) 411-5433

Evansville
SW Indiana Mental Health Center
415 Mulberry Street
Evansville, IN 47713
(812) 423-7791

Fort Wayne
Charter Beacon Behavioral Health
1720 Beacon Street
Fort Wayne, IN 46805
(219) 423-3651
Hotline: (800) 242-7837

Parkview Behavioral Health
1909 Carew Street
Fort Wayne, IN 46805
(219) 484-6636
Hotline: (800) 284-8439

Gary
Gary Community MH Center
1100 West 6th Avenue
Gary, IN 46402
(219) 885-4264

Indianapolis
Family Service Association
615 North Alabama Street
Indianapolis, IN 46204
(317) 634-6341

St. Vincent Hospital
1717 West 86th Street
Indianapolis, IN 46260
(317) 338-4800

Salvation Army Harbor Light Center
927 North Pennsylvania Street
Indianapolis, IN 46204
(317) 639-4118

Kokomo
St. Joseph Hospital
1907 West Sycamore Street
Kokomo, IN 46901
(765) 457-2606
Hotline: (800) 638-7844

Lafayette
New Directions
775 East Street
Lafayette, IN 47905
(765) 589-3318

South Bend
Madison Center Inc.
712 North Niles Avenue
South Bend, IN 46617
(219) 234-0061

Terra Haute
Hamilton Center Inc.
620 8th Avenue
Terra Haute, IN 47804
(812) 231-8323
Hotline: (800) 742-0787

IOWA

Ames
Center for Addictions Recovery
511 Duff Avenue
Ames, IA 50010
(515) 232-3206

Burlington
Alcohol & Drug Dependency Services of
SE Iowa
1340 Mount Pleasant Street
Burlington, IA 52601
(319) 753-6567

Cedar Rapids
Foundation Crisis Center
1540 2nd Avenue SE
Cedar Rapids, IA 52403
(319) 362-2174
Hotline: (800) 332-4224

Des Moines
Substance Abuse Education Program
Grimes Office Building
Des Moines, IA 50319
(515) 281-3021

Iowa Methodist Medical Center
700 East University
Des Moines, IA 50309
(515) 263-2424

Iowa City
Mid Eastern Council on Chemical Abuse
430 Southgate Avenue
Iowa City, IA 52240
(319) 351-4357

Ottumwa
Ottumwa Regional Health Center
312 East Alta Vista Avenue
Ottumwa, IA 52501
(515) 684-3170

Spirit Lake
NW Iowa Alcoholism & Drug Treatment Unit
Dickinson County Memorial Hospital
Spirit Lake, IA 51360
(712) 336-4560

KANSAS

Atchison
Atchison Valley Hope Treatment Center
1816 North 2nd Street
Atchison, KS 66002
(913) 367-1618

Emporia
Mental Health Center
1000 Lincoln Street
Emporia, KS 66801
(316) 342-0548

Garden City
Area Mental Health Center
1111 East Spruce Street
Garden City, KS 67846
(316) 275-0625

Great Bend
Central Kansas Psychological Services
925 Patton Street
Great Bend, KS 67530
(316) 792-6619

Hays
High Plains Mental Health Center
208 East 7th Street
Hays, KS 67601
(785) 628-2871

Hutchinson
Horizons Mental Health Center
1715 East 23rd Avenue
Hutchinson, KS 67502
(316) 665-2240
Hotline: (800) 794-0163

Kansas City
Kansas City Drug & Alcohol Information
707 Minnesota Avenue
Kansas City, KS 66101
(913) 342-3011

Substance Abuse Center of Eastern Kansas
3505 Rainbow Blvd.
Kansas City, KS 66103
(913) 362-0045

Lawrence
Regional Prevention Center of East
Central KS
3312 Clinton Parkway
Lawrence, KS 66047
(913) 841-4138

Manhattan
Pawnee Mental Health Services
423 Houston Street
Manhattan, KS 66502
(913) 587-4315

Newton
Mirror Inc.
130 East 5th Street
Newton, KS 67114
(316) 283-6743

Norton
Valley Hope
103 South Walbash Street
Norton, KS 67654
(785) 877-5111

Shawnee Mission
Charter Hospital
8000 West 127th Street
Shawnee Mission, KS 66213
(913) 897-4999
Hotline: (800) 242-7837

Topeka
Shawnee Community Mental Health
Center
330 SW Oakley Street
Topeka, KS 66606
(785) 234-33448

Shawnee Regional Prevention & Recovery
Services
2209 SW 29th Street
Topeka, KS 66611
(785) 266-8666

Wichita
Parallax Program
3410 East Funston Street
Wichita, KS 67218
(316) 689-6813

Wichita/Sedwick County Regional
Prevention Center
1421 East 2nd Street
Wichita, KS 67214
(316) 262-2421

KENTUCKY

Ashland
Pathways Inc.
1212 Bath Avenue
Ashland, KY 41105
(606) 329-8588
Hotline: (800) 562-8909

Bowling Green
Lifeskills Inc.
1911 Scottsville Road
Bowling Green, KY 42104
(502) 842-5509
Hotline: (800) 223-8913

Corbin
Baptist Regional Medical Center
1 Trillium Way
Corbin, KY 40701
(606) 528-1212
Hotline: (800) 395-4435

Covington
Family Alcohol & Drug Counseling Center
722 Scott Street
Covington, KY 41012
(606) 431-2225

Danville
Bluegrass Prevention Center
1000 Lexington Road
Danville, KY 40422
(606) 236-4245
Hotline: (800) 928-8000

Elizabethtown
Communicare Recovery Center
1311 North Dixie Avenue
Elizabethtown, KY 42701
(502) 765-5145

Frankfort
Bluegrass Prevention Center
1009 Twilight Trail
Frankfort, KY 40601
(502) 875-5740
Hotline: (800) 928-8000

Henderson
Regional Addiction Resources
6347 Highway 60 East
Henderson, KY 42420
(502) 827-2380
(800) 433-7291

Lexington
Bluegrass East Comprehensive Care Center
200 West 2nd Street
Lexington, KY 40507
(606) 281-2100
(800) 928-8000

Charter Ridge Behavioral Health System
3050 Rio Dosa Drive
Lexington, KY 40509
(606) 269-2325
Hotline: (800) 242-7837

Louisville
Baptist Hospital East Chemical
Dependency Program
4000 Kresge Way
Louisville, KY 40207
(502) 896-7135

Ten Broeck Hospital
8521 La Grange Road
Louisville, KY 40242
(502) 426-6380

Wellness Institute
332 West Broadway Street
Louisville, KY 40202
(502) 589-9355

Newport
Comp Care Centers of Northern Kentucky
10th & Monmouth Streets
Newport, KY 41071
(606) 431-4450

Owensboro
River Valley Regional Prevention Center
233 West 9th Street
Owensboro, KY 42301
(502) 686-0036
Hotline: (800) 433-7291

Somerset
Adanta Behavioral Health Services
101 Hardin Lane
Somerset, KY 42501
(606) 679-7348
Hotline: (800) 633-5599

LOUISIANA

Baton Rouge
Alcohol & Drug Abuse Council of Greater
Baton Rouge
1801 Florida Blvd.
Baton Rouge, LA 70802
(504) 343-8330

Behavioral Health Center
3601 North Blvd.
Baton Rouge, LA 70806
(504) 387-7900
Hotline: (800) 375-7575

Salvation Army
7361 Airline Highway
Baton Rouge, LA 70805
(504) 355-4483
Hotline: (800) 435-7504

Houma
Alcohol & Drug Abuse Council of South
Louisiana
813 Belanger Street
Houma, LA 70360
(504) 879-2273
Hotline: (504) 850-8514

Lafayette
Lafayette Alcohol & Drug Abuse Clinic
400 St. Julien Street
Lafayette, LA 70506
(318) 262-5870

Monroe
Southern Oaks Addiction Recovery
4781 South Grand Street
Monroe, LA 71202
(318) 362-5430

New Orleans
Covenant House
611 North Johnson Street
New Orleans, LA 70112
(504) 523-3292
(800) 999-9999

Division of Addictive Disorders
LSU Medical School
1542 Tulane Avenue
New Orleans, LA 70112
(504) 568-4933
Hotline: (504) 568-3931

Methodist Psychiatric Pavilion
5610 Read Blvd.
New Orleans, LA 70127
(504) 244-5661
Hotline: (800) 725-2199

Shreveport
Council on Alcoholism & Drug Abuse of
Northwest Louisiana
840 Jordan Street
Shreveport, LA 71101
(318) 222-8511

Alcohol Dependence Program
510 East Stoner Avenue
Shreveport, LA 71101
(318) 424-6012

Thibodaux
Bayou Council on Alcoholism
504 St. Louis Street
Thibodaux, LA 70301
(504) 446-0643

Winnsboro
Northeast Louisiana Substance Abuse Inc.
210 Main Street
Winnsboro, LA 71295
(318) 435-7558

MAINE

Augusta
Crisis & Counseling Center
99 Western Avenue
Augusta, ME 04330
(207) 626-3448

Bangor
Alternative Choices Counseling
27 State Street
Bangor, ME 04401
(207) 990-5002

Community Health & Counseling Services
900 Hammond Street
Bangor, ME 04401
(207) 947-0366

Outpatient Chemical Dependency Agency
158 Hollow Street
Bangor, ME 04402
(207) 848-2750
Hotline: (800) 640-8839

Lewiston
St. Marys Regional Medical Center
100 Campus Avenue
Lewiston, ME 04243
(207) 777-8100

Tri County Substance Abuse Counseling
Services
Lewiston, ME 04241
(207) 778-3556
Hotline: (207) 783-4680

Portland
Chemical Dependency Recovery Program
980 Forest Avenue
Portland, ME 04103
(207) 780-3577
Hotline: (207) 623-8411

Wellness Health Association
650 Brighton Avenue
Portland, ME 04102
(207) 773-0003

MARYLAND

Annapolis
Anne Arundel County Health Dept.
Addiction Services
2200 Somerville Road
Annapolis, MD 21401
(410) 222-7121

Pathfinder Health Services
2448 Holly Avenue
Annapolis, MD 21401
(410) 266-9494
Hotline: (800) 245-7013

Baltimore
Baltimore County Bureau of Substance
Abuse
401 Washington Avenue
Baltimore, MD 21204
(410) 887-3828

Greater Baltimore Medical Center
1017 East Baltimore Street
Baltimore, MD 21202
(410) 522-7828
Hotline: (410) 522-6571

Johns Hopkins Hospital
911 North Broadway Street
Baltimore, MD 21205
(410) 955-5439

Overcome Substance Abuse Program
3101 Towanda Avenue
Baltimore, MD 21215
(410) 383-4982
Hotline: (410) 383-4357

Total Health Care Inc.
1800 North Charles Street
Baltimore, MD 21201
(410) 361-8100

Belair
Harford County Health Dept.
5 North Main Street
Bel Air, MD 21014
(410) 879-6988

Bethesda
Suburban Hospital
8600 Old Georgetown Road
Bethesda, MD 20814
(301) 896-2522

College Park
Recovery Network
6201 Greenbelt Road
College Park, MD 20740
(301) 345-1919
Hotline: (800) 879-0554

Cumberland
Allegany County Addictions Program
12500 Willowbrook Road SE
Cumberland, MD 21502
(301) 777-5680

Frederick
Frederick County Health Dept. Substance
Abuse Services
300-B Scholls Lane
Frederick, MD 21701
(301) 694-1775

Havre De Grace
Ashley Inc.
800 Tydings Lane
Havre De Grace, MD 21078
(800) 799-4673

Laurel
Mental Health & Addiction Services
7300 Van Dusen Road
Laurel, MD 20707
(301) 497-7980
Hotline: (800) 435-5550

Rockville
Charter Behavioral Health Systems
14901 Broschart Road
Rockville, MD 20850
(301) 251-4652
Hotline: (301) 251-4545

Dept. of Health & Human Services
Other Way Treatment Program
401 Fleet Street
Rockville, MD 20850
(301) 217-1475

Salisbury
Peninsula Regional Medical Center
100 East Carrol Street
Salisbury, MD 21801
(410) 543-7162
Hotline: (410) 543-7160

Silver Spring
Substance Abuse Prevention
Dept. of Health & Human Services
8630 Fenton Street
Silver Spring, MD 20910
(301) 217-1116
Hotline: (301) 656-9161

Westminster
Carroll County Health Dept.
Addiction Treatment Services
290 South Center Street
Westminster, MD 21157
(410) 876-4410

MASSACHUSETTS

Beverly
North Shore Counseling Center
23 Broadway Street
Beverly, MA 01915
(508) 922-2280

Boston
After Care Services Inc.
1A Monmouth Avenue
Boston, MA 02128
(617) 569-4561

Boston Alcohol & Substance Abuse
Programs
30 Winter Street
Boston, MA 02108
(617) 482-5292

Boston Public Health Commission
Addiction Services
723 Massachusetts Avenue
Boston, MA 02118
(617) 534-4212

Bridge Over Troubled Waters
47 West Street
Boston, MA 02111
(617) 423-9575

South Boston Action Council
424 West Broadway
Boston, MA 02127
(617) 269-5160

Spaulding Rehabilitation Hospital
125 Nashua Street
Boston, MA 02114
(617) 720-6991

Brockton
Brockton Hospital Substance Abuse
Services
680 Center Street
Brockton, MA 02402
(508) 941-7000

Dorchester
First Inc.
321 Blue Hill Avenue
Dorchester, MA 02121
(617) 445-5230 •
Hotline: (617) 445-1500

Fall River
Stanley Street Treatment & Resources
386 Stanley Street
Fall River, MA 02720
(508) 679-5222

Falmouth
Gosnold Counseling Center
196 Ter Heun Drive
Falmouth, MA 02540
(508) 548-7118

Framingham
South Middlesex Opportunity Council
300 Howard Street
Framingham, MA 01701
(508) 620-2682

Gloucester
Health & Education Services
298 Washington Street
Gloucester, MA 01930
(978) 282-0296

Holyoke
Providence Hospital
317 Maple Street
Holyoke, MA 01040
(413) 535-1000
Hotline: (800) 274-7724

Jamaica Plain
Faulkner Hospital
1153 Center Street
Jamaica Plain, MA 02130
(617) 983-7709

Lawrence
Arbour Counseling Services
599 Canal Street
Lawrence, MA 01840
(508) 686-8202

Lowell
Family Service of Greater Lowell
97 Central Street
Lowell, MA 01852
(508) 937-3000

Lynn
Lynn Community Health Center
269 Union Street
Lynn, MA 01901
(617) 581-3900

New Bedford
Center for Health & Human Services
105 William Street
New Bedford, MA 02740
(508) 996-3147

North Adams
North Adams Regional Hospital
Hospital Avenue
North Adams, MA 01247
(413) 664-5368

Pittsfield
Berkshire Medical Center
165 Tor Court
Pittsfield, MA 01201
(413) 442-1400
Hotline: (800) 222-1664

Plymouth
Center for Health & Human Services
71 Christa McAuliffe Blvd.
Plymouth, MA 02360
(508) 746-6737

Quincy
Bay State Community Services
15 Cottage Avenue
Quincy, MA 02169
(617) 471-8400

Roxbury
Dimock Community Health Center
55 Dimock Street
Roxbury, MA 02119
(617) 442-8801

Salem
Salem Hospital
172 Lafayette Street
Salem, MA 01970
(508) 744-4033
Hotline: (508) 741-1200

Somerville
Cambridge Public Health Alliance
Addiction Services
26 Central Street
Somerville, MA 02143
(617) 625-8900
Hotline: (800) 825-4357

Springfield
Child & Family Service
367 Pine Street
Springfield, MA 01105
(413) 737-1426

Northern Educational Services
756 State Street
Springfield, MA 01109
(413) 737-8523

Waltham
Middlesex Regional Addiction Treatment
Center
775 Trapelo Road
Waltham, MA 02154
(617) 894-0004

Worcester
Adcare Hospital Substance Abuse
Treatment Program
107 Lincoln Street
Worcester, MA 01605
(508) 799-9000
Hotline: (800) 345-3552

Community Healthlink
12 Queen Street
Worcester, MA 01610
(508) 860-1200

MICHIGAN

Ann Arbor
Ann Arbor Community Center
625 North Main Street
Ann Arbor, MI 48104
(734) 662-3128

Child & Family Services of Washtenaw
3879 Packard Street
Ann Arbor, MI 48108
(313) 973-1900

Battle Creek
Substance Abuse Council of Greater Battle Creek
35 West Michigan Avenue
Battle Creek, MI 49017
(616) 968-4699

Bay City
Bay Haven Chemical Dependency &
Mental Health Programs
713 9th Street
Bay City, MI 48708
(517) 894-3799

Birmingham
Substance Abuse Prevention Coalition
870 Bowers Street
Birmingham, MI 48009
(810) 826-8600

Brighton
Brighton Hospital
12851 East Grand River Street
Brighton, MI 48116
(810) 227-1211

Clinton Township
Salvation Army Harbor Light Center
42590 Stepnitz Drive
Clinton Township, MI 48036
(810) 954-1838

Dearborn
Family Services of Wayne County
19855 West Outer Drive
Dearborn, MI 48124
(313) 274-5840

Detroit
Aurora Community Programs
15738 Grand River Street
Detroit, MI 48227
(313) 838-1849

Family Services of Wayne County
220 Bagley Street
Detroit, MI 48226
(313) 965-2141

Genesis House
3840 Fairview Street
Detroit, MI 48214
(313) 579-0417

National Council on Alcoholism & Drug
Dependence
2927 West McNichols Street
Detroit, MI 48221
(313) 341-9891
Hotline: (800) 388-9891

Northeast Guidance Center
2670 Chalmers Street
Detroit, MI 48215
(313) 824-5620

Salvation Army Harbor Light Center
2643 Park Avenue
Detroit, MI 48201
(313) 964-0577

Farmington Hills
Farmington Area Counseling Centers
23450 Middlebelt Road
Farmington Hills, MI 48336
(248) 477-6767

Flint
Insight Recovery Center
1110 Eldon Baker Drive
Flint, MI 48507
(810) 744-3600
Hotline: (800) 356-4357

National Council on Alcoholism & Addictions
202 East Boulevard Drive
Flint, MI 48503
(810) 767-0350

Grand Rapids
Family Outreach Center
1939 South Division Avenue
Grand Rapids, MI 49507
(616) 247-3815

Kent Community Hospital
Longford Careunit
750 Fuller Avenue NE
Grand Rapids, MI 49503
(616) 336-2400

Salvation Army
1931 Boston Street SE
Grand Rapids, MI 49506
(616) 235-1565

Hancock
Upper Michigan Behavioral Health Services
1045 Quincy Street
Hancock, MI 49930
(906) 487-9377
Hotline: (800) 562-9753

Holland
Child & Family Services
412 Century Lane
Holland, MI 49423
(616) 396-2301

Jackson
Family Service & Children's Aid
330 West Michigan Avenue
Jackson, MI 49201
(517) 787-7920

National Council on Alcoholism
950 West Munroe Street
Jackson, MI 49202
(517) 782-2580

Kalamazoo
Gateway Villa
1910 Shaffer Road
Kalamazoo, MI 49001
(616) 382-9820

Mid-America Psychological Services
5630 Holiday Terrace
Kalamazoo, MI 49009
(616) 327-1438

Lansing
National Council on Alcoholism & Drug
Dependence
913 West Holmes Road
Lansing, MI 48910
(517) 394-1252
Hotline: (800) 344-3400

Sparrow Outpatient Behavioral Health
Services
1210 West Saginaw Street
Lansing, MI 48915
(517) 377-0542

Livonia
Northwestern Community Services
18316 Middlebelt Road
Livonia, MI 48152
(248) 615-9730
Hotline: (313) 224-7000

Marquette
Marquette General Hospital
420 West Magnetic Street
Marquette, MI 49855
(906) 225-3160
Hotline: (906) 225-3994

Midland
Focus Substance Abuse Counseling &
Information Center
4604 North Saginaw Road
Midland, MI 48640
(517) 631-7992
Hotline: (517) 631-4550

Monroe
Monroe County Community Health
123-125 West First Street
Monroe, MI 48161
(313) 243-7340

Petoskey
Northern MI Community Mental Health
Dual Diagnosis Program
1040 Bayview Road
Petoskey, MI 49770
(616) 348-3096
Hotline: (800) 442-7315

Pontiac
Oakland Family Services
114 Orchard Lake Road
Pontiac, MI 48341
(248) 858-7766

Saginaw
Dot Caring Centers
1915 Fordney Street
Saginaw, MI 48601
(517) 752-6198
Hotline: (800) 822-7464

Health Source Saginaw Pathway
3340 Hospital Road
Saginaw, MI 48603
(517) 790-7750

Southfield
Tri County Drug & Substance Abuse
Prevention
28551 Southfield Road
Southfield, MI 48076
(810) 559-1990

Traverse City
Addiction Treatment Services
116 East 8th Street
Traverse City, MI 49684
(616) 922-4810
Hotline: (800) 622-4810

Troy
Troy Community Coalition for the
Prevention of Alcohol Abuse
1100 Urbancrest Street
Troy, MI 48083
(248) 740-0431

Warren
Bi County Counseling Center
26091 Sherwood Street
Warren, MI 48091
(810) 758-2872
Hotline: (810) 307-9100

West Bloomfield
Henry Ford Health Systems
6773 West Maple Road
West Bloomfield, MI 48322
(248) 661-6100

MINNESOTA

Anoka
Anoka/Metro Regional Treatment Center
3300 4th Avenue North
Anoka, MN 55303
(612) 576-5533

Austin
Austin Medical Center
101 14th Street
Austin, MN 55912
(507) 433-7389
Hotline: (800) 422-1295

Bemidji
Upper MN Mental Health Center
722 15th Street
Bemidji, MN 56601
(218) 751-3280
Hotline: (800) 422-0045

Brainerd
Brainerd Regional Human Services Center
1777 Highway 18 East
Brainerd, MN 56401
(218) 828-2387

Burnsville
River Ridge Treatment Center
1510 East 122nd Street
Burnsville, MN 55337
(612) 894-7722

Center City
Hazelden Foundation
15245 Pleasant Valley Road
Center City, MN 55012
(612) 257-4010

Crookston
Glenmore Recovery Program
323 South Minnesota Street
Crookston, MN 56716
(218) 281-9511
(800) 584-9226

Duluth
Miller Dawn Medical Center
502 East 2nd Street
Duluth, MN 55805
(218) 720-1356

Eden Prairie
Northern Healthcare Associates
14400 Martin Drive
Eden Prairie, MN 55344
(612) 934-7554
Hotline: (800) 547-7433

Fergus Falls
Fergus Falls Regional Treatment Center
Fergus Falls, MN 56537
(218) 739-7348

Grand Rapids
Northland Recovery Center
1215 7th Avenue SE
Grand Rapids, MN 55744
(218) 327-1105
Hotline: (218) 326-7788

Minneapolis
Fairview Recovery Services
2450 Riverside Avenue
Minneapolis, MN 55454
(612) 672-2222

Hazelden Center for Youth & Families
11505 36th Avenue North
Minneapolis, MN 55441
(612) 509-3873
Hotline: (800) 257-7800

Health Recovery Center
3255 Hennepin Avenue South
Minneapolis, MN 55408
(612) 827-7800
Hotline: (800) 247-6237

Salvation Army Harbor Light
1010 Currie Avenue North
Minneapolis, MN 55405
(612) 338-0113

Rochester
Mayo Clinic
200 SW 1st Street
Rochester, MN 55905
(507) 255-4065

Zumbro Valley Mental Health Center
1932 Viking Drive NW
Rochester, MN 55906
(507) 281-6240
Hotline: (507) 281-6248

Saint Cloud
Central Minnesota Mental Health Center
1321 13th Street
Saint Cloud, MN 56303
(612) 252-5010
Hotline: (800) 253-5555

Saint Cloud Hospital
1406 North 6th Avenue
Saint Cloud, MN 56303
(612) 255-5613
Hotline: (800) 742-4357

Saint Paul
Twin Town Treatment Center
1706 University Avenue
Saint Paul, MN 55104
(612) 645-3661

United Hospital
333 North Smith Avenue
Saint Paul, MN 55102
(612) 220-8639

Thief River Falls
Glenmore Recovery
621 North Labree Avenue
Thief River Falls, MN 56701
(218) 681-8019
Hotline: (800) 584-9226

Winona
Hiawatha Valley Mental Health Center
166 Main Street
Winona, MN 55987
(507) 454-4341
Hotline: (800) 657-6777

MISSISSIPPI

Biloxi
Gulf Oaks Hospital
180-C DeBuys Road
Biloxi, MS 39535
(601) 388-0600

Columbus
Baptist Memorial Hospital
525 Willowbrook Road
Columbus, MS 39703
(601) 244-2161

Gulfport
Sand Hill Hospital
11150 Highway 49 North
Gulfport, MS 39503
(601) 831-1700
Hotline: (800) 831-1700

Jackson
Charter Behavioral Health System
3531 East Lakeland Drive
Jackson, MS 39296
(601) 939-9030
Hotline: (800) 242-7837

Mississippi Baptist Medical Center
1225 North State Street
Jackson, MS 39201
(601) 968-1102
Hotline: (800) 378-7613

National Council on Alcoholism & Drug
Dependency
333 North Mart Plaza
Jackson, MS 39206
(601) 366-6880

Laurel
South Central Regional Medical Center
1220 Jefferson Street
Laurel, MS 39441
(601) 426-4000
Hotline: (800) 262-1711

Meridian
Laurel Wood Center
5000 Highway 39 North
Meridian, MS 39303
(601) 483-6211
Hotline: (800) 422-5563

Mooreville
Mental Health Center
Route 1
Mooreville, MS 38857
(601) 844-3531

Vicksburg
Marian Hill
100 McAuley Drive
Vicksburg, MS 39180
(601) 631-2700

MISSOURI

Boonville
Boonville Valley Hope
1415 Ashley Road
Boonville, MO 65233
(660) 882-6547

Columbia
Family Counseling Center
117 North Garth Street
Columbia, MO 65203
(573) 449-2581

Farmington
SE Missouri Community Treatment Center
5536 State Highway 32
Farmington, MO 63640
(573) 756-5749
Hotline: (800) 455-5749

Gladstone
Columbia Health Systems
6910 North Holmes Street
Gladstone, MO 64118
(816) 468-6700

Hannibal
Hannibal Council on Alcohol & Drug Abuse
146 Communications Drive
Hannibal, MO 63401
(314) 248-1196

Hayti
Family Counseling Center
Highway 3
Hayti, MO 63851
(573) 359-2600

Joplin
Ozark Center
3006 McClelland Blvd.
Joplin, MO 64803
Hotline: (800) 247-0661

Kansas City
National Council on Alcoholism & Drug
Dependence
633 East 63rd Street
Kansas City, MO 64110
(816) 361-5900

Swope Parkway Comp Health Center
3950 East 51st Street
Kansas City, MO 64130
(816) 923-5800

Two Rivers Psychiatric Hospital
5121 Raytown Road
Kansas City, MO 64133
(816) 356-5688
Hotline: (816) 358-4357

Western Missouri Mental Health Center
600 East 22nd Street
Kansas City, MO 64108
(816) 512-4000

Kennett
Family Counseling Center
925 Highway VV
Kennett, MO 63857
(573) 888-5925

Kirksville
Preferred Family Healthcare
1101 South Jamison Street
Kirksville, MO 63501
(660) 665-1962

Park Hills
SE Missouri Community Treatment Center
528 East Main Street
Park Hills, MO 63601
(573) 431-0554
Hotline: (800) 455-5749

Saint Joseph
Family Guidance Center
1120 Main Street
Saint Joseph, MO 64501
(816) 236-2626
Hotline: (800) 892-5750

Saint Louis
Hyland Center
10020 Kennerly Road
Saint Louis, MO 63128
(314) 525-4400
Hotline: (800) 525-2032

National Council on Alcoholism & Drug Abuse
8790 Manchester Road
Saint Louis, MO 63144
(314) 962-3456

Safety Council of Greater St. Louis
1015 Locust Street
Saint Louis, MO 63101
(314) 621-9200

St. Louis Comprehensive Health Center
5917 Martin Luther King Drive
Saint Louis, MO 63112
(314) 381-0560
Hotline: (800) 967-0146

Springfield
Center for Addictions
1423 North Jefferson Avenue
Springfield, MO 65802
(417) 836-3269

Lakeland Regional Hospital
440 South Market Street
Springfield, MO 65806
(417) 865-5581
Hotline: (800) 432-1210

Safety Council of the Ozarks
1111 South Glenstone Street
Springfield, MO 65804
(417) 869-2121

MONTANA

Billings
Rimrock Foundation
1231 North 29th Street
Billings, MT 59101
(406) 248-3175

Bozeman
Alcohol & Drug Services of Gallatin
County
502 South 19th Street
Bozeman, MT 59715
(406) 586-5493
Hotline: (800) 262-2463

Deer Lodge
Chemical Dependency & Family
Counseling
304 Milwakee Avenue
Deer Lodge, MT 59722
(406) 846-3442

Great Falls
Rocky Mountain Treatment Center
920 4th Avenue North
Great Falls, MT 59401
(406) 727-8832

Helena
Boyd Andrew Chemical Dependency Care
Center
Arcade Building
Helena, MT 59624
(406) 443-2343

Marion
Wilderness Treatment Center
200 Hubbart Dam Road
Marion, MT 59925
(406) 854-2832

Miles City
Eastern Montana Mental Health Services
2200 Box Elder
Miles City, MT 59301
(406) 232-6542

Missoula
St. Patrick Hospital
500 West Broadway
Missoula, MT 59802
(406) 327-3020

Western Montana Regional Mental Health
500 North Higgins Street
Missoula, MT 59802
(406) 543-8623

NEBRASKA

Columbus
Mid-East Nebraska Behavioral Health Care
Services
3314 26th Street
Columbus, NE 68601
(402) 564-1426
Hotline: (800) 586-3050

Grand Island
Central Nebraska Council on Alcoholism
219 West 2nd Street
Grand Island, NE 68801
(308) 384-7365

Hastings
Council on Alcoholism & Drugs
432 North Minnesota Avenue
Hastings, NE 68901
(402) 463-0524

Lincoln
Alcohol & Drug Information
Clearinghouse
650 J Street
Lincoln, NE 68508
(402) 474-1992
Hotline: (800) 648-4444

Lincoln General Hospital
1650 Lake Street
Lincoln, NE 68502
(402) 473-5268
Hotline: (800) 742-7845

Lincoln Valley Hope Alcohol Counseling
& Referral Center
3633 O Street
Lincoln, NE 68510
(402) 477-3677
Hotline: (800) 544-5101

Norfolk
Odyssey Counseling Services
401 South 17th Street
Norfolk, NE 68701
(402) 371-7215

North Platte
Heartland Counseling & Consulting Clinic
110 North Bailey Street
North Platte, NE 69101
(3308) 534-6029
Hotline: (308) 534-6963

Omaha
Methodist Richard Young Behavioral Unit
415 South 25th Avenue
Omaha, NE 68131
(402) 354-6600
Hotline: (800) 782-3160

Mental Health Administration
1941 South 42nd Street
112 Applewood Mall
Omaha, NE 68105
(402) 444-6573

South Omaha Alcoholism Counseling Agency
2900 O Street
Omaha, NE 68107
(402) 734-3000

Oneill
Valley Hope
1421 North 10th Street
Oneill, NE 68763
(402) 336-3747

Scottsbluff
Panhandle Mental Health Center
4110 Avenue D
Scottsbluff, NE 69361
(308) 635-3171

NEVADA

Carson City
Community Counseling Center
625 Fairview Drive
Carson City, NV 89701
(702) 882-3945

Elko
Ruby View Counseling Center
401 Railroad Street
Elko, NV 89803
(702) 738-8004

Fallon
Churchill Council on Alcohol & Other Drugs
165 North Carson Street
Fallon, NV 89406
(702) 423-1412
Hotline: (800) 232-6382

Las Vegas
Bridge Counseling Associates
1701 West Charleston Blvd.
Las Vegas, NV 89102
(702) 474-6450

Clark County Health District Addiction
Treatment Clinic
625 Shadow Lane
Las Vegas, NV 89127
(702) 383-1347

Westcare Inc.
930 North 4th Street
Las Vegas, NV 89101
(702) 383-4044
Hotline: (702) 385-3330

Reno
Family Counseling Services
777 Sinclair Street
Reno, NV 89501
(702) 329-0623

Reno Treatment Center
750 Kuenzli Street
Reno, NV 89502
(702) 333-5233

NEW HAMPSHIRE

Concord
Community Alcohol Information Program
261 Sheep Davis Drive
Concord, NH 03301
(603) 228-8181

Merrimack County Alcohol & Drug
Intervention Program
48 Branch Turnpike
Concord, NH 03301
(603) 228-1959
Hotline: (800) 852-3388

Dover
Southeastern New Hampshire Services
272 County Farm Road
Dover, NH 03820
(603) 749-3981
Hotline: (800) 698-7647

Dublin
Marathon House
1 Pierce Road
Dublin, NH 03444
(603) 563-8107

Keene
Monadnock Substance Abuse Services
310 Marlboro Street
Keene, NH 03431
(603) 357-3007
Hotline: (603) 357-5270

Laconia
Lakes Region General Hospital
80 Highland Street
Laconia, NH 03246
(603) 524-3211

Manchester
Bedford Counseling Associates
25 South River Road
Manchester, NH 03100
(603) 623-1916

National Council on Alcoholism & Drug
Dependence
93-101 Manchester Street
Manchester, NH 03101
(603) 625-4528

Nashua
Greater Nashua Council on Alcoholism
Pine Street Extension
Nashua, NH 03060
(603) 880-1894

Portsmouth
Child & Family Services
1 Junkins Avenue
Portsmouth, NH 03801
(603) 772-3786

NEW JERSEY

Absecon
Family Service Association of Atlantic
County
312 East Whitehorse Pike
Absecon, NJ 08201
(609) 652-2377

Atlantic City
Associates for Life Enhancement
26 South New York Avenue
Atlantic City, NJ 08401
(609) 345-8722
Hotline: (800) 356-2909

Blairstown
Little Hill/Alina Lodge
Ward Road
Paulinskill, NJ 07825
(908) 362-6114

Bridgetown
Cumberland County Alcoholism & Drug
Abuse Services
72 North Pearl Street
Bridgetown, NJ 08302
(609) 451-3727

Camden
Substance Abuse Center of Southern Jersey
413-417 Broadway Street
Camden, NJ 08103
(609) 757-9190

Cape May Court House
Cape May Council on Alcoholism & Drug Abuse
6 Moore Road
Cape May Court House, NJ 08210
(609) 465-2282

East Orange
Substance Abuse Program
60 Halstead Street
East Orange, NJ 07018
(973) 266-5200

Elizabeth
Seton Center for Chemical Dependency
225 Williamson Street
Elizabeth, NJ 07207
(908) 353-8830

Flemington
National Council on Alcoholism & Drug
Dependence
89 Park Avenue
Flemington, NJ 08822
(908) 782-3909

Hackensack
Bergen County Division of Family Guidance
21 Main Street
Hackensack, NJ 07602
(201) 599-6235

Jersey City
National Council on Alcoholism & Drug Abuse
83 Wayne Street
Jersey City, NJ 07302
(201) 451-2877
Hotline: (201) 451-2974

Lakewood
Alcoholism & Drug Abuse Council
1195 Route 70
Lakewood, NJ 08701
(908) 367-5515

Morristown
Morris County Addiction Recovery Center
30 Schuyler Place
Morristown, NJ 07963
(201) 285-6990

New Brunswick
Program for Addictions
254 Easton Avenue
New Brunswick, NJ 08903
(732) 745-8688

Newark
Integrity Inc.
103 Lincoln park
Newark, NJ 07102
(201) 974-7315
Hotline: (888) 660-4488

Newton
Sussex Council on Alcohol & Drug Abuse
49 High Street
Newton, NJ 07860
(973) 383-4787

Paramus
Bergen County Council on Alcoholism &
Drug Abuse
Bergen Pines Hospital Complex
Paramus, NJ 07652
(201) 261-2183

Paterson
Barnert Memorial Hospital Center
680 Broadway Street
Paterson, NJ 07514
(201) 977-6704

Phillipsburg
Warren Hospital Alcohol Recovery Center
185 Roseberry Street
Phillipsburg, NJ 08865
(908) 859-6787
Hotline: (908) 859-6700

Plainfield
Organizations for Recovery
519 North Avenue
Plainfield, NJ 07060
(908) 769-4700
Hotline: (908) 412-2732

Princeton
Family Service of Central NJ
120 John Street
Princeton, NJ 08542
(609) 924-2098

Seabrook
Seabrook House
Polk Lane
Seabrook, NJ 08302
(609) 455-7575
Hotline: (800) 582-5968

Somerville
Somerset Council on Alcoholism & Drug
Dependency
34 West Main Street
Somerville, NJ 08876
(908) 722-4900

Toms River
Alternatives Counseling Center
96 East Water Street
Toms River, NJ 08754
(908) 286-4242

Trenton
Greater Trenton Community MH Center
132 North Warren Street
Trenton, NJ 08607
(609) 396-6788

Mercer Council on Alcoholism & Drug
Addiction
408 Bellevue Avenue
Trenton, NJ 08618
(609) 396-5874
Hotline: (800) 322-5525

NEW MEXICO

Albuquerque
Counseling & Psychotherapy Institute
803 Tijeras Street NW
Albuquerque, NM 87194
(505) 243-2223

Presbyterian Alcohol & Drug Treatment Center
8300 Constitution Street NE
Albuquerque, NM 87110
(505) 291-2555

Western Clinical Health Services
4105 Silver Street
Albuquerque, NM 87108
(505) 262-1538

Carlsbad
Carlsbad Mental Health Association
914 North Canal Street
Carlsbad, NM 88220
(505) 885-4836
Hotline: (505) 885-8888

Farmington
Presbyterian Medical Services
1001-D West Broadway Street
Farmington, NM 87499
(505) 325-0238
Hotline: (505) 599-5176

Gallup
Rehoboth McKinley Health Care Services
650 Vanden Bosch Parkway
Gallup, NM 87301
(505) 722-3804
Hotline: (505) 722-0007

Sante Fe
St. Vincent Hospital
455 St. Michaels Drive
Sante Fe, NM 87501
(505) 820-5276

Silver City
Border Area Mental Health Services
315 South Hudson Street
Silver City, NM 88062
(505) 388-4412
Hotline: (800) 426-0997

NEW YORK

Albany
Albany Citizens Council on Alcoholism
334 Broadway Street
Albany, NY 12207
(518) 434-2367
Hotline: (518) 465-7388

Albany County Substance Abuse
Prevention Program
845 Central Avenue
Albany, NY 12206
(518) 437-1390
Hotline: (518) 447-9650

Hope House Inc.
445 New Karner Road
Albany, NY 12205
(518) 456-8043

St. Peters Addiction Recovery Center
315 South Manning Blvd.
Albany, NY 12208
(518) 525-1307

Albion
Unity Behavioral Health
168 South Main Street
Albion, NY 14411
(716) 589-0055

Batavia
Genesee Council on Alcohol & Substance Abuse
30 Bank Street
Batavia, NY 14020
(716) 343-9620
Hotline: (716) 343-3131

Binghamton
Broome County Drug Awareness Center
168 Water Street
Binghamton, NY 13901
(607) 778-1251

United Health Services Wilson Memorial
Hospital
Mitchell Avenue
Binghamton, NY 13903
(607) 762-2452
Hotline: (607) 762-2257

Bronx
Bronx Citizens Committee Inc.
Alcohol Crisis Center
1668 Webster Avenue
Bronx, NY 10457
(718) 716-4200
Hotline: (888) 716-4200

Bronx/Lebanon Hospital Center
321 East Tremont Avenue
Bronx, NY 10457
(718) 518-3700

Hunts Point Multi Service
630 Jackson Avenue
Bronx, NY 10455
(718) 993-3010

Promesa Inc.
1776 Clay Avenue
Bronx, NY 10457
(718) 299-1100
Hotline: (888) 513-7464

Brooklyn
Coney Island Hospital
2601 Ocean Parkway
Brooklyn, NY 11235
(718) 616-5664

Cumberland Diagnostic & Treatment Center
100 North Portland Avenue
Brooklyn, NY 11205
(718) 260-7644

Long Island College Hospital
339 Hicks Street
Brooklyn, NY 11201
(718) 780-1120

New Directions
202-206 Flatbush Avenue
Brooklyn, NY 11217
(718) 398-0800

Buffalo
Erie County Council for the Prevention of
Alcoholism
220 Delaware Avenue
Buffalo, NY 14202
(716) 852-1781

Health Care Plan Inc.
899 Main Street
Buffalo, NY 14203
(716) 878-2700

Canandaigua
Ontario County Dept. of Substance Abuse
Services
3907 County Road 46
Canandaigua, NY 14424
(716) 396-4190

Canastota
Madison County Council Alcohol Abuse
Information & Referral Program
Rural Route 5
Canastota, NY 13032
(315) 697-3947
Hotline: (315) 697-3949

Carmel
Arms Acres
Seminary Hill Road
Carmel, NY 10512
(914) 225-3400

Putnam Family & Community Services
47 Brewster Avenue
Carmel, NY 10512
(914) 225-2700

Clifton Springs
Finger Lakes Alcoholism Referral Agency
28 East Main Street
Clifton Springs, NY 14432
(315) 462-7070

Cobleskill
Schoharie County Council on Alcoholism
& Substance Abuse
150 East Main Street
Cobleskill, NY 12043
(518) 234-8705

Corning
Steuben Council on Alcoholism
27 Denison Parkway
Corning, NY 14830
(607) 937-5156

East Hampton
Program Planned for Life
95 Industrial Road
East Hampton, NY 11937
(516) 537-2891
Hotline: (800) 982-7300

East Meadow
Nassau County Dept. of Drug & Alcohol
Addiction
2201 Hempstead Turnpike
East Meadow, NY 11554
(516) 572-5922

Ellenville
Ulster County Mental Health Services
50 Center Street
Ellenville, NY 12428
(914) 647-3266

Elmira
Alcohol & Drug Abuse Council of
Chemung County
380 West Gray Street
Elmira, NY 14905
(607) 734-1567

Flushing
Elmhurst Hospital Center Alcoholism Clinic
79-01 Broadway Street
Flushing, NY 11373
(718) 334-4600

Freeport
South Shore Child Guidance Center
87 Church Street
Freeport, NY 11520
(516) 378-2992

Gloversville
Alcoholism & Substance Abuse Council
40 North Main Street
Gloversville, NY 12078
(518) 725-8464

Happauge
Suffolk Coalition To Prevent Alcohol &
Drug Dependence
900 Wheeler Road
Happauge, NY 11788
(516) 366-1717

Hempstead
Hempstead General Hospital Medical Center
800 Front Street
Hempstead, NY 11550
(516) 560-1429
(800) 933-3869

Huntington Station
Suffolk County Dept. of Alcohol &
Substance Abuse
689 East Jericho Turnpike
Huntington Station, NY 11746
(516) 854-4400

Ithaca
Alcohol Recovery Services
201 East Green Street
Ithaca, NY 14850
(607) 274-6288

Jamaica
Creedmoor Alcoholism Treatment Center
80 Winchester Blvd.
Jamaica, NY 11427
(718) 264-3740

Queens Hospital Center
82 164th Street
Jamaica, NY 11432
(718) 883-2750

Jamestown
Chautauga Alcohol & Substance Abuse Council
2-6 East 2nd Street
Jamestown, NY 14701
(716) 664-3608

Kingston
Ulster County Mental Health Services
239 Golden Hill lane
Kingston, 12401
(914) 340-4000
Hotline: (914) 338-2370

Monticello
Sullivan County Mental Health
Alcoholism Services
217 Broadway Street
Monticello, NY 12701
(914) 791-4550

Newburgh
Orange County Dept. of Mental Health
104 2nd Street
Newburgh, NY 12550
(914) 565-4960

New Rochelle
United Hospital
3 The Boulevard
New Rochelle, NY 10801
(914) 235-6633

New York
Alcoholism Council of Greater New York
352 Park Avenue South
New York, NY 10010
(212) 979-6277
Hotline: (212) 252-7001

Beth Israel Medical Center
380 2nd Avenue
New York, NY 10010
(212) 614-6100

Harlem Hospital
506 Lennox Avenue
New York, NY 10037
(212) 939-1000

Harlem YMCA Substance Abuse
Prevention Program
180 West 135th Street
New York, NY 10030
(212) 281-4100

Hazelden New York
233 East 17th Street
New York, NY 10003
(212) 490-9522

NY Center for Addiction Treatment
Services
568 Broadway
New York, NY 10012
(212) 966-9537

North General Hospital
1879 Madison Avenue
New York, NY 10035
(212) 423-4000

Saint Lukes/Roosevelt Hospital Center
324 West 108th Street
New York, NY 10025
(212) 280-0100

Niagara Falls
Alcoholism Council in Niagara County
800 Main Street
Niagara Falls, NY 14301
(716) 282-1228

Nyack
Rockland Council on Alcoholism
11 Division Avenue
Nyack, NY 10960
(914) 358-4357
Hotline: (914) 353-5665

Olean
Cattaraugus County Council on
Alcoholism & Substance Abuse
201 South Union Street
Olean, NY 14760
(716) 373-5202

Plainview
Nassau County Dept. of Drug & Alcohol
Addiction
1425 Old Country Road
Plainview, NY 11803
(516) 572-8520

Plattsburgh
Clinton County Alcoholism Services
16 Ampersand Drive
Plattsburgh, NY 12901
(518) 562-2780

Poughkeepsie
Dutchess County Substance Abuse Clinic
20 Manchester Road
Poughkeepsie, NY 12603
(914) 486-2950
Hotline: (914) 486-2700

Riverhead
North Suffolk Mental Health Center
1149 Old Country Road
Riverhead, NY 11901
(516) 369-5588

Rochester
Family Service of Rochester
30 North Clinton Avenue
Rochester, NY 14604
(716) 232-1840

National Council on Alcoholism
1 Mount Hope Avenue
Rochester, NY 14620
(716) 423-9490

Saratoga Springs
Saratoga County Alcoholism Services
254 Church Street
Saratoga Springs, NY 12866
(518) 587-8800

Schenectady
Alcoholism Council of Schenectady County
302 State Street
Schenectady, NY 12305
(518) 346-4436

Staten Island
Bayley Seton Hospital
75 Vanderbilt Avenue
Staten Island, NY 10304
(718) 390-5065

Staten Island University Hospital
376 Seguine Avenue
Staten Island, NY 10309
(718) 356-8910
Hotline: (718) 226-2801

Syracuse
Crouse Hospital
410 South Crouse Avenue
Syracuse, NY 13210
(315) 470-7314

Onondaga Council on Alcoholism
716 East Washington Street
Syracuse, NY 13210
(315) 471-1359

Troy
Rensselaer County Substance Abuse Services
7th Avenue
Troy, NY 12180
(518) 270-2800

Utica
Insight House Chemical Dependency Services
500 Whitesboro Street
Utica, NY 13502
(315) 724-5168
(888) 546-5224

Watertown
Alcohol & Substance Abuse Council of
Jefferson County
302 Globe Mall Court Street
Watertown, NY 13601
(315) 788-4660

White Plains
New York Hospital
Cornell Medical Center
21 Bloomingdale Road
White Plains, NY 10605
(914) 682-9100

Yonkers
Yonkers General Hospital
2 Park Avenue
Yonkers, NY 10703
(914) 964-7972

NORTH CAROLINA

Asheville
Blue Ridge Center
283 Biltmore Avenue
Asheville, NC 28801
(704) 252-8748
Hotline: (704) 252-4357

Burlington
Alamance Caswell Area Substance Abuse
Program
319 North Graham-Hopedale Road
Burlington, NC 27217
(336) 513-4200

Charlotte
Information & Referral Service
301 South Brevard Street
Charlotte, NC 28202
(704) 377-1100

Mecklenburg County Area Substance
Abuse Services
429 Billingsley Road
Charlotte, NC 28211
(704) 336-2023

Durham
Durham Council on Alcoholism & Drug
Dependency
3109 University Drive
Durham, NC 27707
(919) 493-3114

Greensboro
Alcohol & Drug Services
5209 West Wendover Avenue
Greensboro, NC 27404
(336) 812-8645

Guildford County Substance Abuse Program
201 North Eugene Street
Greenboro, NC 27401
(336) 373-4981
Hotline: (336) 373-4993

Greenville
Pitt County Substance Abuse Treatment
Services
203 Government Circle
Greenville, NC 27834
(252) 413-1600

Morganton
Burke Council on Alcoholism
203 White Street
Morganton, NC 28655
(704) 43-1221

Raleigh
Charter Behavioral Health System
3019 Falstaff Road
Raleigh, NC 27610
(919) 250-7000
Hotline: (800) 242-7837

Winston Salem
Charter Behavioral Health System
3637 Old Vineyard Road
Winston Salem, NC 27104
(336) 768-7710

NORTH DAKOTA

Bismarck
Burleigh County Detoxification Center
514 East Thayer Avenue
Bismarck, ND 58501
(701) 222-6651

Fargo
Drake & Burau Counseling Services
1202 23rd Street South
Fargo, ND 58103
(701) 293-5429
Hotline: (701) 237-7335

Southeast Human Service Center
2624 9th Avenue South
Fargo, ND 58103
(701) 298-4500

Grand Forks
Northeast Human Service Center
1407 24th Avenue South
Grand Forks, ND 58201
(701) 795-3000

Jamestown
South Central Human Service Center
520 3rd Street NW
Jamestown, ND 58401
(701) 253-6300
Hotline: (701) 253-6304

Minot
North Central Human Service Center
400 22nd Avenue NW
Minot, ND 58701
(701) 857-8500

OHIO

Akron
Akron Health Dept. Counseling Services
177 South Broadway Street
Akron, OH 44308
(216) 375-2984

Family Services of Summit County
212 East Exchange Street
Akron, OH 44304
(330) 376-9494

Canton
Crisis Intervention Center
2421 13th Street NW
Canton, OH 44708
(216) 452-9812
Hotline: (330) 452-6000

Chardon
Ravenwood Mental Health Center
12557 Ravenwood Drive
Chardon, OH 44024
(440) 285-3568
Hotline: (888) 285-5665

Cincinnati
Alcoholism Council of Cincinnati Area
118 William Howard Taft Road
Cincinnati, OH 45219
(513) 281-7880

Talbert House
328 McGregor Avenue
Cincinnati, OH 45219
(513) 684-7968

Cleveland
Community Assessment Foundation
5163 Broadway Avenue
Cleveland, OH 44127
(216) 441-0200

Cuyahoga County Alcohol Outpatient
Treatment
1276 West 3rd Street
Cleveland, OH 44113
(216) 443-8250

St. John West Shore Hospital
2351 East 22nd Street
Cleveland, OH 44115
(216) 835-6059
Hotline: (800) 686-4673

Columbus
Columbus Area Community Mental
Health Center
3035 West Broad Street
Columbus, OH 43204
(614) 252-0711

Columbus Area Council on Alcoholism
360 South 3rd Street
Columbus, OH 43215
(614) 464-0191

North Central Mental Health Services
3035 West Broad Street
Columbus, OH 43204
(614) 351-3450

Dayton
Center for Alcohol & Drug Addiction Services
600 Wayne Avenue
Dayton, OH 45410
(513) 461-5223

South Community Inc.
8353 Yankee Street
Dayton, OH 45458
(937) 438-4444
Hotline: (937) 435-6660

Defiance
Five County Alcohol & Drug Program
418 Auglaize Street
Defiance, OH 43512
(419) 782-9920
Hotline: (800) 468-4357

Galion
Community Counseling Services
269 Portland Way South
(419) 468-3010
Hotline: (800) 755-9010

Hamilton
Alcohol & Chemical Abuse Council
240 Fair Avenue
Hamilton, OH 45011
(513) 868-2100

Lima
St. Ritas Medical Center
730 West Market Street
Lima, OH 45801
(419) 226-9029
Hotline: (800) 567-4673

Lisbon
Columbiana County Mental Health Center
40722 State Route 154
Lisbon, OH 44432
(216) 424-9573

Lorain
Lakeland Institute
205 West 20th Street
Lorain, OH 44052
(216) 233-1067

Mansfield
Center for Individual & Family Services
741 Scholl Road
Mansfield, OH 44907
(419) 756-1717
Hotline: (419) 522-4357

Marion
Marion Area Counseling Center
320 Executive Drive
Marion, OH 43302
(614) 387-5210
Hotline: (614) 383-2273

Middletown
Behavioral Counseling Services
1001 Reinatz Blvd.
Middletown, OH 45042
(513) 424-3505
Hotline: (513) 523-4146

Newark
Licking County Alcoholism Prevention Program
62 East Steven Street
Newark, OH 43055
(740) 366-7303

Painesville
Lake Geauga Center on Alcoholism
796 Oak Street
Painesville, OH 44077
(440) 354-2848
Hotline: (440) 951-3511

Sandusky
Bayshore Counseling Services
1218 Cleveland Road
Sandusky, OH 44870
(419) 626-9156

Springfield
Alcohol & Drug Abuse Programs for Treatment
825 East High Street
Springfield, OH 45501
(513) 323-0951

Toledo
Comprehensive Addiction Service Systems
2465 Collingswood Blvd.
Toledo, OH 43620
(419) 241-8827

Toledo Hospital
2142 North Cove Blvd.
Toledo, OH 43606
(419) 471-2300

Waverly
Pike County Recovery Council
196 East Emmitt Avenue
Waverly, OH 45690
(740) 947-7581

Youngstown
Mahoning County Chemical Dependency
Programs
527 North Meridian Road
Youngstown, OH 44509
(330) 797-0070
Hotline: (330) 747-5111

OKLAHOMA

Ardmore
Mental Health Services of Southern
Oklahoma
2530 South Commerce Street
Ardmore, OK 73401
(580) 226-5048
Hotline: (800) 522-1090

Cushing
Valley Hope
100 South Jones Avenue
Cushing, OK 74023
(918) 225-1736

Lawton
Jim Taliaferro Community Mental Health Center
602 SW 38th Street
Lawton, OK 73505
(580) 248-5780

Miami
Northeastern Oklahoma Council on Alcoholism
316 Eastgate Blvd.
Miami, OK 74355
(918) 542-2845

Oklahoma City
Community Counseling Center
1140 North Hudson Street
Oklahoma City, OK 73103
(405) 272-0660
Hotline: (405) 271-5050

Oklahoma County Crisis Intervention Center
1200 NE 13th Street
Oklahoma City, OK 73117
(405) 271-6800
Hotline: (800) 522-9054

Referral Center for Alcohol & Drug
Service of Central Oklahoma
1215 NW 25th Street
Oklahoma City, OH 73106
(405) 525-2525

Tulsa
Community Service Council
1430 South Boulder Street
Tulsa, OK 74119
(918) 585-5551
Hotline: (918) 836-4357

New Choice
4833 South Sheridan Road
Tulsa, OK 74145
(918) 663-6057

Tulsa Regional Medical Center
744 West 9th Street
Tulsa, OK 74127
(918) 599-5880

OREGON

Albany
Addiction Counseling & Education Services
1856 Grand Prairie Road SE
Albany, OR 97321
(503) 967-6597

Eugene
Addiction Counseling & Education Services
84 Centennial Loop
Eugene, OR 97401
(541) 344-2237

Prevention & Recovery Northwest
1188 Olive Street
Eugene, OR 97401
(541) 484-9274

Hillsboro
Washington County Treatment Program
245A SE 5th Street
Hillsboro, OR 97123
(503) 640-1715

Newport
Lincoln County Council on Alcohol &
Drug Abuse
155 SW High Street
Newport, OR 97365
(503) 265-2971
Hotline: (541) 265-3559

Portland
Behavioral Health Division
421 SW 6th Avenue
Portland, OR 97204
(503) 248-5464
Hotline: (503) 232-8083

Project for Community Recovery
3525 NE Martin Luther King Jr. Blvd.
Portland, OR 97212
(503) 281-2804

Tualatin Valley Centers
4531 SE Belmont Street
Portland, OR 97215
(503) 234-3400

Roseburg
Council on Alcohol & Drug Abuse
Prevention & Treatment
621 West Madrone Street
Roseburg, OR 97470
(541) 672-2691

Salem
Inside Out Care Inc.
780 Commercial Street SE
Salem, OR 97302
(503) 585-3423

Marion County Health Dept.
3180 Center Street NE
Salem, OR 97301
(503) 588-5358
Hotline: (503) 585-4949

PENNSYLVANIA

Aliquippa
Gateway Rehabilitation Center
Moffet Run Road
Aloquippa, PA 15001
(412) 766-8700

Allentown
Council on Alcohol & Drug Abuse
126 North 9th Street
Allentown, PA 18102
(610) 437-0801

Allenwood
White Deer Run
Devitt Camp Road
Allenwood, PA 17810
(717) 538-2567
(800) 255-2335

Altoona
Blair County Community Action Program
2100 6th Avenue
Altoona, PA 16612
(814) 946-3651

Athens
Bradford County Drug & Alcohol
419 South Main Street
Athens, PA 18810
(717) 888-6657
Hotline: (800) 332-6718

Bellefonte
Central Single County Authority
Substance Abuse Education
420 Holmes Street
Bellefonte, PA 16823
(814) 355-6782
(800) 643-5432

Butler
Butler Memorial Hospital
911 East Brady Street
Butler, PA 16001
(724) 284-4357
Hotline: (800) 831-2468

Chambersburg
Franklin/Fulton County Alcohol Program
425 Franklin Farm Road
Chambersburg, PA 17201
(717) 263-1256
Hotline: (800) 994-2555

Chester
Crozer Chester Medical Center
2600 West 9th Street
Chester, PA 19013
(610) 497-7416
Hotline: (610) 447-7600

Doylestown
Council on Alcoholism & Drug Abuse
252 West Swamp Road
Doylestown, PA 18901
(215) 345-6644
Hotline: (800) 221-6333

Erie
Drug & Alcohol Services Network
809 Peach Street
Erie, PA 16501
(814) 459-4581
Hotline: (814) 870-5424

Exton
Chester County Council on Addictive Diseases
930 East Lancaster Avenue
Exton, PA 19341
(610) 363-6164
Hotline: (800) 917-1117

Harrisburg
Harrisburg Area Counseling Services
3907 Derry Street
Harrisburg, PA 17111
(717) 558-8510

Lancaster
Lancaster County Council on Alcohol &
Drug Abuse
630 Janet Avenue
Lancaster, PA 17601
(717) 299-2831
Hotline: (717) 393-4673

Lebanon
Lebanon County Crisis Intervention
4th & Walnut Street
Lebanon, PA 17042
(717) 274-3363

Media
Family & Community Service
100 West Front Street
Media, PA 19063
(610) 566-7540

New Castle
Drug & Alcohol Community Treatment Centers
332 Highland Avenue
New Castle, PA 16101
(724) 658-2696

New Kensington
Family Services of Western PA
One Kensington Square
New Kensington, PA 15068
(724) 339-7180

Norristown
Montgomery County Emergency Services
50 Beech Drive
Norristown, PA 19401
(610) 279-6100
Hotline: (800) 452-4189

Philadelphia
Abbotsford Community Health Center
3205 Defense Terrace
Philadelphia, PA 19129
(215) 843-9720

Belmont Center for Comprehensive Treatment
4200 Monument Road
Philadelphia, PA 19131
(215) 581-3757
Hotline: (800) 220-4357

Diagnostic & Rehabilitation Center
229 Arch Street
Philadelphia, PA 19106
(215) 625-8060

Intercommunity Action Inc.
6122 Ridge Avenue
Philadelphia, PA 19128
(215) 487-1330

Pittsburgh
St. Francis Central Hospital
1200 Center Avenue
Pittsburgh, PA 15219
(412) 562-3267

Salvation Army Harbor Light Center
865 West North Avenue
Pittsburgh, PA 15233
(412) 231-0500

Reading
Center for Mental Health
6th & Spruce Streets
Reading, PA 19611
(610) 378-6186

West Grove
Southern Chester County Medical Center
1011 West Baltimore Pike
West Grove, PA 19390
(610) 869-1500

Wilkes-Barre
Family Service Association of Wyoming Valley
31 West Market Street
Wilkes-Barre, PA 18701
(717) 823-5144
Hotline: (800) 432-8007

RHODE ISLAND

Newport
CODAC Inc.
93 Thames Street
Newport, RI 02840
(401) 846-4150

Pawtucket
Rhode Island Council on Alcoholism & Drug
Dependence
500 Prospect Street
Pawtucket, RI 02860
(401) 725-0410
Hotline: (800) 622-7422

Providence
Family Service Inc.
55 Hope Street
Providence, RI 02906
(401) 331-1350

Roger Williams Medical Center
825 Chalkstone Avenue
Providence, RI 02908
(401) 456-2363
Hotline: (800) 252-6466

Talbot Treatment Division
520 Hope Street
Providence, RI 02905
(401) 464-2129
Hotline: (401) 274-7111

Warwick
Kent County Mental Health Center
300 Centerville Road
Warwick, RI 02886
(401) 738-1760

Woonsocket
Road Counseling
8 Court Street
Woonsocket, RI 02895
(401) 762-7000
Hotline: (401) 272-7111

SOUTH CAROLINA

Aiken
Commission on Alcohol & Drug Abuse
1105 Gregg Highway
Aiken, SC 29801
(803) 649-1900
Hotline: (803) 648-9900

Anderson
Alcohol & Drug Abuse Commission
226 McGee Road
Anderson, SC 29625
(864) 260-4168
Hotline: (864) 604-0168

Beaufort
Beaufort County Alcohol & Drug Abuse Dept.
1905 Duke Street
Beaufort, SC 29902
(843) 525-7407

Charleston
Dept. of Alcohol & Other Drug Services
615 Wesley Drive
Charleston, SC 29417
(843) 769-7112
Hotline: (843) 722-0100

Columbia
Alcohol & Drug Abuse Council
1325 St. Julian Place
Columbia, SC 29169
(803) 733-1390
Hotline: (803) 256-3100

Conway
Horry County Commission on Alcohol &
Drug Abuse
1004 Bell Street
Conway, SC 29526
(843) 248-6291

Greenville
Commission on Alcohol & Drug Abuse
3336 Old Buncombe Road
Greenville, SC 29617
(864) 467-3737

Lancaster
Commission on Alcohol & Drug Abuse
114 South Main Street
Lancaster, SC 29720
(803) 285-6912

Marion
Alcohol & Drug Abuse Program
103 Court Street
Marion, SC 29571
(843) 423-8292

Rock Hill
Commission on Alcohol & Drug Abuse
199 South Herlong Avenue
Rock Hill, SC 29732
(803) 324-1800

Spartanburg
Commission on Alcohol & Drug Abuse
131 North Spring Street
Spartanburg, SC 29306
(864) 582-7588
Hotline: (864) 596-2300

Winnsboro
Substance Abuse Commission
200 Calhoun Street
Winnsboro, SC 29180
(803) 635-2335

SOUTH DAKOTA

Aberdeen
Northern Alcohol/Drug Referral &
Information Center
221 South First Street
Aberdeen, SD 57402
(605) 225-6131
Hotline: (605) 622-5800

Mitchell
Community Alcohol/Drug Center
901 South Miller Street
Mitchell, SD 57301
(605) 995-3780

Rapid City
County Alcohol & Drug Program
725 North Lacrosse Street
Rapid City, SD 57701
(605) 394-6128

Sioux Falls
Carroll Institute Alcohol & Drug Center
310 South 1st Avenue
Sioux Falls, SD 57104
(605) 336-2556
Hotline: (605) 332-9257

Southeast Alcohol Prevention Resource Center
908 West Avenue North
Sioux Falls, SD 57104
(605) 367-4293

Watertown
Human Service Agency Alcohol Referral
& Treatment Center
123 19th Street NE
Watertown, SD 57201
(605) 886-7602
Hotline: (605) 886-0123

Yankton
Human Services Center
3515 Broadway Avenue
Yankton, SD 57078
(605) 668-3280

TENNESSEE

Chattanooga
Council for Alcohol & Drug Abuse Services
207 Spears Avenue
Chattanooga, TN 37405
(423) 756-7644

Gallatin
Cumberland Mental Health Services
528 East Main Street
Gallatin, TN 37066
(615) 452-1354

Jackson
Council on Alcoholism & Drug Dependency
900 East Chester Street
Jackson, TN 38301
(901) 423-3656

Knoxville
Knox County Counseling & Recovery
Services
2247 Western Avenue
Knoxville, TN 37921
(423) 546-3500

Memphis
Memphis Alcohol & Drug Council
1430 Poplar Avenue
Memphis, TN 38104
(901) 274-0056

St. Joseph Hospital
220 Overton Street
Memphis, TN 38105
(901) 577-2902
Hotline: (901) 577-3700

Southeast Mental Health Center
2579 Douglas Street
Memphis, TN 38114
(901) 369-1400

Nashville
Alcohol & Drug Council
2912 Westwood Drive
Nashville, TN 37204
(615) 269-0029

Cumberland Heights Alcohol Treatment
8283 River Road
Nashville, TN 37209
(615) 352-1757
Hotline: 356-2700

Oak Ridge
Methodist Medical Center
990 Oak Ridge Turnpike
Oak Ridge, TN 37830
(423) 481-1409
Hotline: (423) 481-1680

TEXAS

Abilene
Abilene Regional Mental Health Center
2616 Clack Street
Abilene, TX 79606
(915) 690-5147

Amarillo
Amarillo Council on Alcohol & Drug Abuse
616 North Polk Street
Amarillo, TX 79107
(806) 374-6688
Hotline: (800) 566-6688

Austin
Austin Drug & Alcohol Abuse Program
7801 North Lamar Street
Austin, TX 78729
(512) 454-8180

Austin Mental Health Center
3000 Oak Springs Drive
Austin, TX 78702
(512) 926-5301

Salvation Army Rehab Center
4216 South Congress Avenue
Austin, TX 78745
(512) 447-2272
Hotline: (512) 323-1899

Beaumont
Jefferson County COADA
700 North Street
Beaumont, TX (409) 835-4989
Hotline: (800) 221-8328

Bryan
Brazos Valley Council on Alcohol & Drug Abuse
1103 Turkey Creek
Bryan, TX 77801
(409) 776-7070

Center
Alcohol & Drug Abuse Council
114 Hurst Street
Center, TX 75935
(409) 634-5853

Clarksville
Northeast Texas Council on Alcohol & Drug Abuse
200 Walnut Road
Clarksville, TX 75426
(903) 737-4394
Hotline: (800) 221-2992

Corpus Christi
Coastal Bend Council on Alcohol & Drug Abuse
10110 Compton Road
Corpus Christi, TX 78418
(512) 884-3436

Dallas
Baylor University Medical Center
3500 Gaston Avenue
Dallas, TX 75246
(214) 820-7676
Hotline: (800) 828-8880

Green Oaks at Medical City
7808 Clodus Fields Drive
Dallas, TX 75251
(214) 991-9504

Salvation Army Social Service Center
5302 Harry Hines Blvd.
Dallas, TX 75235
(214) 688-4494

El Paso
Aliviane Inc.
2130 Mills Street
El Paso, TX 79901
(915) 779-3764

West Texas Council on Alcoholism & Drug Abuse
215 Willow Street
El Paso, TX 79901
(915) 577-0791

Fort Worth
Family Services Inc.
1424 Hemphill Street
Fort Worth, TX 76104
(817) 927-8884
Hotline: (817) 927-5544

Tarrant Council on Alcoholism & Drug Abuse
1701 West Freeway
Fort Worth, TX 76102
(817) 332-6329

Georgetown
Williamson County Council on Alcohol &
Drug Abuse
707 Main Street
Georgetown, TX 78627
(512) 869-2571

Greenville
Crossroads Council on Alcohol & Drug Abuse
2612 Jordan Street
Greenville, TX 75401
(903) 455-5438
Hotline: (903) 457-8383

Houston
Cypress Creek Hospital
205 Hollow Tree Lane
Houston, TX 77090
(281) 586-7600

Houston Council on Alcohol & Drug Abuse
3333 Eastside Street
Houston, TX 77098
(713) 520-5502

Memorial Hospital Southwest
7600 Beechnut Street
Houston, TX 77074
(713) 776-5070

Volunteers of America Inc.
308 East Rogers Street
Houston, TX 77022
(713) 692-8190

Huntsville
Montgomery/Walker County COADA
526 11th Street
Huntsville, TX 77340
(409) 291-7433
Hotline: (800) 324-2557

Laredo
South Texas Council on Alcohol & Drug Abuse
1502 Laredo Street
Laredo, TX 78040
(956) 791-6131

Longview
East Texas Council on Alcoholism & Drug Abuse
450 East Loop 281
Longview, TX 75605
(903) 753-7633
Hotline: (800) 441-8639

Lubbock
Lubbock Regional Mental Health Center
1602 10th Street
Lubbock, TX 79401
(806) 766-0237

Lufkin
Alcohol & Drug Abuse Council
304 North Raguet Street
Lufkin, TX 75901
(409) 634-5753

Midland
Glenwood Hospital
3300 South Fm 1788
Midland, TX 79711
(915) 563-1200

Paris
Northeast Texas Council on Alcohol & Drug Abuse
136 Grand Avenue
Paris, TX 75460
(903) 737-4394
Hotline: (800) 221-2992

San Angelo
Alcohol & Drug Abuse Council
1021 Caddo Street
San Angelo, TX 76901
(915) 655-9641
Hotline: (800) 880-9641

San Antonio
Alamo Mental Health Group
5115 Medical Drive
San Antonio, TX 78229
(210) 616-0074

Community Counseling Center
Stanley Road
San Antonio, TX 78234
(210) 221-0221

Sherman
Texoma Council on Alcoholism & Drug Abuse
103 South Travis Street
Sherman, TX 75090
(903) 892-9911

Stafford
Fort Bend Regional Council on Alcohol &
Drug Abuse
10435 Greenbough Street
Stafford, TX 77477
(281) 261-1370
Hotline: (281) 342-8828

Texarkana
Red River Council on Alcohol & Drug Abuse
2101 Dudley Street
Texarkana, TX 75502
(501) 774-7962
Hotline: (800) 793-7171

Victoria
Bay Area Council on Drugs & Alcohol Inc.
3708 North Navarro Street
Victoria, TX 77901
(281) 280-0800
Hotline: (800) 510-3111

Waco
Freeman Center
1515 Columbus Avenue
Waco, TX 76701
(254) 753-3625

UTAH

Delta
Central Utah Counseling Center
51 North Center
Delta, UT 84624
(435) 864-3073

Farmington
Davis County Mental Health Center
291 South 200 West
Farmington, UT 84025
(801) 451-7799
Hotline: (801) 773-7060

Ogden
Utah Alcoholism Foundation
529 25th Street
Ogden, UT 84401
(801) 392-5971

Park City
Valley Mental Health
1753 Sidewinder Drive
Park City, UT 84060
(435) 649-8347

Provo
Utah County Human Services
100 East Center Street
Provo, UT 84606
(801) 370-8427

Salt Lake City
Community Counseling Center
660 South 200 East
Salt Lake City, UT 84101
(801) 355-2846

Salt Lake County Division of Substance Abuse
2001 South State Street
Salt Lake City, UT 84190
(801) 468-2009

Utah Alcoholism Foundation
1006 East 100 South
Salt Lake City, UT 84102
(801) 359-8374

Utah State Division of Substance Abuse
120 North 200 West
Salt Lake City, UT 84103
(801) 538-9836

VERMONT

Bennington
United Counseling Service
Ledge Hill Drive
Bennington, VT 05201
(802) 442-5491

Brattleboro
Alcohol & Substance Abuse Program
75 Linden Street
Brattleboro, VT 05301
(802) 257-7785

Burlington
Vermont Office of Alcohol & Drug Abuse
Programs
108 Cherry Lane
Burlington, VT 05402
(802) 651-1550

Morrisville
Lamoille County Mental Health Services
Washington County Highway
Morrisville, VT 05661
(802) 888-4914

Newport
Northeast Kingdom Mental Health Services
103 Main Street
Newport, VT 05855
(802) 334-5246

South Burlington
Fletcher Allen
200 Twin Oaks Terrace
South Burlington, VT 05403
(802) 865-3333

VIRGINIA

Alexandria
Alexandria Community Services
2355-A Mill Road
Alexandria, VA 22314
(703) 329-2020

Arlington
Arlington County Alcohol & Drug Program
1725 North George Mason Drive
Arlington, VA 22205
(703) 358-4900

Chesapeake
Chesapeake Substance Abuse Program
524 Albermarie Drive
Chesapeake, VA 23320
(757) 547-3336

Clintwood
Dickenson County Community Services
McClure Avenue
Clintwood, VA 24228
(703) 926-1680

Danville
Danville Regional Medical Center
142 South Main Street
Danville, VA 24541
(804) 799-4450
Hotline: (800) 258-7741

Leesburg
Loudoun County Mental Health Center
102 Heritage Way NE
Leesburg, VA 20175
(703) 771-5100

Newport News
Woodside Hospital
17579 Warwick Blvd.
Newport News, VA 23603
(800) 697-0999

Norfolk
Norfolk Community Services Board
1150 East Little Creek Road
Norfolk, VA 23518
(757) 441-1899

Richmond
Richmond Behavioral Health Authority
900 East Marshall Street
Richmond, VA 23219
(804) 780-5876

Roanoke
Division of Substance Abuse Services
301 Elm Street
Roanoke, VA 24016
(703) 345-9841
Hotline: (540) 981-9351

Virginia Beach
Counseling & Assistance Center
NAS Oceana
Virginia Beach, VA 25460
(757) 433-3433

Winchester
Northwestern Community Services Board
158 Front Royal Road
Winchester, VA 22602
(703) 667-8888
Hotline: (540) 667-0145

WASHINGTON

Bellevue
Coastal Treatment Services
12443 Bel Red Road
Bellevue, WA 98005
(425) 646-4406

Bellingham
Unitycare Inc.
202 Unity Street
Bellingham, WA 98225
(360) 647-2341
Hotline: (800) 640-2599

Bremerton
Kitsap Mental Health Services
5455 Alimira Drive
Bremerton, WA 98311
(206) 479-4994

Chewelah
Stevens County Counseling Services
East 301 Clay Street
Chewelah, WA 99109
(509) 684-4597
Hotline: (800) 767-6091

Dayton
Columbia County Services
221 East Washington Street
Dayton, WA 99328
(509) 382-2527

Everett
Lakeside Milam Recovery Centers
2731 Wetmore Avenue
Everett, WA 98201
(425) 259-0796

Issaquah
Lakeside Milam Recovery Centers
22525 SE 64th Place
Issaquah, WA 98027
(425) 392-8468

Kent
South King County Recovery Centers
505 South Washington Avenue
Kent, WA 98032
(206) 854-6513

Kirkland
Lakeside Milam Recovery Centers
10322 NE 132nd Street
Kirkland, WA 98034
(425) 823-3116
Hotline: (800) 232-1559

Longview
Lower Columbia Council on Substance Abuse
1260 Commerce Avenue
Longview, WA 98632
(360) 577-7105

Monroe
Drug Abuse Council of Snohomish County
909 West Main Street
Monroe, WA 98272
(360) 794-5077

Olympia
Alcohol & Drug Abuse program
700 North Lilly Road NE
Olympia, WA 98506
(206) 472-3200
Hotline: (888) 287-2680

Othello
Counseling Services of Adam County
165 North First Street
Othello, WA 99344
(509) 488-5611

Seattle
Alcohol/Drug 24 Hour Help Line
3700 Rainier Avenue South
Seattle, WA 98144
(206) 722-3703
Hotline: (206) 722-3700

Lakeside Milam Recovery Centers
12845 Ambaum Blvd. SW
Seattle, WA 98146
(425) 241-0890

South King County Recovery Centers
15025 4th Avenue SW
Seattle, WA 98166
(206) 242-3506

Spokane
Lakeside Recovery Centers
601 West Mallon Street
Spokane, WA 99201
(509) 328-5234

Spokane Addiction Recover Centers
1508 West 6th Street
Spokane, WA 99204
(509) 624-3251

Spokane Regional Health District
1101 West College Avenue
Spokane, WA 99201
(509) 324-1420

Tacoma
Don Mercer Group Behavioral Center
4301 South Pine Street
Tacoma, WA 98409
(253) 476-9826
Hotline: (888) 287-2680

Lakeside Milam Recovery Centers
535 Dock Street
Tacoma, WA 98402
(253) 272-2242
Hotline: (800) 232-1559

Vancouver
Clark County Council on Alcohol & Drugs
509 West 8th Street
Vancouver, WA 98660
(360) 696-1631

Yakima
AJ Consultants
32 North 3rd Street
Yakima, WA 98901
(509) 248-0133
Hotline: (800) 922-2015

WEST VIRGINIA

Charleston
Southway Outpatient Program
1097 Fledder John Road
Charleston, WV 25314
(304) 345-9203
Hotline: (800) 992-3010

Fairmont
Valley Comprehensive Community Mental
Health Center
28 Oakwood Road
Fairmont, WV 26554
(304) 366-7174
Hotline: (800) 232-0020

Martinsburg
Alcohol & Drug Treatment Program
Route 9 South
Martinsburg, WV 25401
(304) 263-0811

Parkersburg
Fellowship Home Inc.
1030 George Street
Parkersburg, WV 26101
(304) 485-3341

Ripley
Westbrook Health Services
6003 Church Street
Ripley, WV 25271
(304) 372-6833
Hotline: (800) 579-5844

Terra Alta
Shawnee Hills Inc.
State Route 1
Terra Alta, WV 26764
(304) 789-2405
Hotline: (800) 282-2405

WISCONSIN

Algoma
Kewaunee County Community Programs
522 4th Street
Algoma, WI 54201
(414) 487-5231
Hotline: (920) 487-5231

Appleton
St. Elizabeths Hospital
1506 South Oneida Street
Appleton, WI 54915
(920) 738-2389
Hotline: (920) 722-7707

Ashland
Ashland County Information & Referral Service
206 6th Avenue West
Ashland, WI 54806
(715) 682-5207

Baraboo
Sauk County Dept. of Human Services
505 Broadway Street
Baraboo, WI 53959
(608) 355-4202
Hotline: (800) 533-5692

Brookfield
Elmbrook Memorial Hospital
19333 West North Avenue
Brookfield, WI 53045
(414) 785-2233

Chippewa Falls
Council on Alcohol & Other Drug Abuse
404 North Bridge Street
Chippewa Falls, WI 54729
(715) 723-1101
Hotline: (800) 428-8159

Eau Claire
Lutheran Social Services
3136 Craig Road
Eau Claire, WI 54701
(715) 838-9856

Friendship
Adams County Dept. of Community Programs
108 East North Street
Friendship, WI 53934
(608) 339-7881

Green Bay
Brown County Mental Health Center
2900 St. Anthony Drive
Green Bay, WI 54311
(920) 391-4700
Hotline: (920) 436-8888

Hayward
Sawyer County Information & Referral Center
105 East 4th Street
Hayward, WI 54843
(715) 634-8270

Janesville
Lutheran Social Services
205 North Main Street
Janesville, WI 53545
(608) 752-7935

Kenosha
Alcohol & Other Drugs Council
1115 56th Street
Kenosha, WI 53140
(414) 658-8166
Hotline: (414) 657-7188

La Crosse
Coulee Council on Alcohol & Other Chemical Abuse
921 West Avenue South
La Crosse, WI 54601
(608) 784-4177

Madison
Mental Health Center of Dane County
625 West Washington Avenue
Madison, WI 53703
(608) 251-2341

Prevention & Intervention Center
2000 Fordem Avenue
Madison, WI 53704
(608) 246-7600

Manitowoc
Human Services Dept. Counseling Center
339 Reed Avenue
Manitowoc, WI 54220
(920) 683-4300
Hotline: (920) 323-2448

Milwaukee
Children & Family Services
4365 North 27th Street
Milwaukee, WI 53216
(414) 536-4400
Hotline: (414) 271-3123

Genesis Behavioral Services
5310 West Capital Drive
Milwaukee, WI 53216
(414) 447-8851

Milwaukee Council on Alcoholism & Drug
Dependence
1126 South 70th Street
Milwaukee, WI 53214
(414) 276-8487
Hotline: (414) 271-3123

Racine
Crisis Center of Racine
1925 Washington Street
Racine, WI 53403
(414) 637-9898

Sheboygan
Sheboygan County Human Services
1011 North 8th Street
Sheboygan, WI 53081
(920) 459-3151

Stevens Point
Family Crisis Center
1616 West River Drive
Stevens Point, WI 54481
(715) 345-6511
Hotline: (800) 472-3377

Waukesha
Council on Alcohol & Other Drug Abuse
327 South Street
Waukesha, WI 53186
(414) 524-7920

Wautoma
Alcoholism & Drug Abuse Services
310 South Scott Street
Wautoma, WI 54982
(920) 787-4656
Hotline: (800) 472-3377

WYOMING

Buffalo
Northern Wyoming Mental Health Center
521 West Lott Street
Buffalo, WY 82834
(307) 684-5531

Cheyenne
Southeast Wyoming Mental Health Center
1920 Thomes Street
Cheyenne, WY 82001
(307) 632-9361

Laramie
Southeast Wyoming Mental Health Center
710 Garfield Street
Laramie, WY 82070
(307) 745-8915
Hotline: (307) 721-3299

Newcastle
Northern Wyoming Mental Health Center
420 Deanne Avenue
Newcastle, WY 82701
(307) 746-4456

Rawlins
Carbon County Counseling Center
721 West Maple Street
Rawlins, WY 82301
(307) 324-7156

Rock Springs
Southwest Counseling Center
1414 9th Street
Rock Springs, WY 82901
(307) 353-6685
Hotline: (307) 353-6677

Sheridan
Northern Wyoming Mental Health Center
1221 West 5th Street
Sheridan, WY 82801
(307) 674-4405

Worland
Washakie County Mental Health Services
509 Big Horn Avenue
Worland, WY 82401
(307) 347-6165

APPENDIX

Ideally, all patients in primary health care settings should be screened for alcohol problems to determine if alcohol is the cause of their illness. A short screen test in a primary health care setting could save an alcoholic years of physical deterioration while their alcoholism goes undetected. The following alcohol screening tests are used to identify problem drinking patterns. There is ongoing research to determine which tests give the best results to all sectors of the population. All tests, however they are worded, have the same objective - to determine if a person has a drinking problem.

CAGE: An Alcoholism Screening Test

- Have you ever felt you should Cut down on your drinking ?
- Have people Annoyed you by criticizing your drinking?
- Have you ever felt bad or Guilty about your drinking?
- Have you ever had a drink first thing in the morning to steady your nerves or to get rid of a hangover (i.e. as an Eye opener)?

Two positive answers to these questions are considered a positive test and indicate that further assessment is warranted. (Source: Adapted from Ewing. 1984.)

RAPS: The Rapid Alcohol Problems Screen

- Do you sometimes take a drink in the morning when you first get up?

- During the past year, has a friend or family member ever told you about things you said or did while you were drinking that you could not remember?
- During the past year, have you had a feeling of guilt or remorse after drinking?
- During the past year, have you failed to do what was normally expected of you because of drinking?
- During the past year, have you lost friends or girl friends or boyfriends because of drinking?

A positive answer to one of the questions is considered a positive test. (Source: Adapted from Cherpitel. 1995.)

Determining Quantity and Frequency of Alcohol Consumption (This quantity/frequency test is currently used by many physicians.)

- On average, how many days per week do you drink alcohol?
- On a typical day when you drink, how many drinks do you have?
- What is the maximum number of drinks you have had on any given occasion during the past month?

Men who drink more than 14 drinks per week or more than 4 drinks per occasion and women who drink more than 7 drinks per week or more than 3 drinks per occasion may be at risk for alcohol-related problems. These people should be assessed further to determine the nature and extent of their alcohol-related problems. (Source: Adapted from National Institute on Alcohol Abuse and Alcoholism. 1995.)

GLOSSARY

AA
(Alcoholics Anonymous)
A group of recovering alcoholics who help each other stay sober. Uses a Twelve Step Program of recovery.

AA Member
Any person who calls himself or herself an AA member.

AA Meeting
Two or more alcoholics meeting together for the purposes of sobriety. Meetings can be either closed - attended only by individuals who have a desire to stop drinking, or open - attended by alcoholics and those who have an interest in alcoholism and AA.

AIDS
Acquired Immunodeficiency Syndrome.

Al-Anon
A support group for those who care about an alcoholic. Uses a Twelve Step Program.

Alcohol Abuser
A person who abuses alcohol and may, or may not, be dependent on alcohol.

Alcohol Dependent
A person who is dependent on alcohol - also termed an alcoholic.

Alcoholic
A person who is dependent on alcohol and suffers from the disease of alcoholism.

Alcoholism
A primary, chronic, progressive and potentially fatal disease. A person with alcoholism is physically dependent on alcohol and has a strong compulsion to drink.

Arrhythmia
An irregular heart rhythm.

BAC
Blood Alcohol Content - used to measure the amount of alcohol in the body and whether a person is legally intoxicated or not.

Blackout
An alcohol-induced period of amnesia during which a person is fully awake. Not to be confused with passing out.

Cardiomyopathy
A general term for primary noninflammatory disease of the heart muscle, the myocardium.

Chronic
Long lasting.

Cirrhosis of liver   Scar tissue replaces normal liver tissue and is accompanied by a decline in liver function. Cirrhosis is the most advanced form of alcoholic liver injury.

Codependent   A person close to the alcoholic who loses his or her own identity in a reaction to the alcoholic's alcoholism.

Defense   An excuse designed to relieve negative feelings brought on by unacceptable behavior caused by drinking.

Denial   Refusing to accept one's alcohol abuse and/or alcoholism.

Detoxification   The process of ridding the body of alcohol.

DUI   Driving Under the Influence (of alcohol.) Also referred to as DWI - Driving While Intoxicated.

Enabler   A person who enables, or assists.

Enabling   The behavior of others that protects the alcoholic from the consequences of his or her drinking and allows him or her to continue drinking.

Family Disease   A disease such as alcoholism which affects the entire family unit and has a steadily deteriorating effect on each member.

Follow-up Care   Continuing the recovery process begun in treatment, typically including therapy with possible individual counseling, and involvement in support groups.

Higher Power   Term used by AA and affiliated self-help groups to explain the spiritual side of recovery. It may, but does not have to, have traditional religious associations. Can mean any spiritual feeling.

HIV   Human Immunodeficiency Virus.

Intervention   Where a group of concerned people meet the alcoholic face to face with the goal of getting him or her to be evaluated by a professional trained in alcoholism and following through on the recommendation of the evaluation.

Pancreatitis   Inflammation of the pancreas.

Primary Disease Alcoholism is a primary disease and not just a symptom of some underlying disorder.

Rational Recovery (RR) Support group for alcoholics focusing on their own powerlessness and incompetence that leads to persistent drinking. RR members are encouraged to limit the number of meetings they attend to avoid gaining a dependency on the group.

Recovering Alcoholic A person who having once been an active drinking alcoholic becomes a non drinker.

Recovery The process of getting emotionally, physically, mentally and spiritually well after years of drinking.

Relapse Return to drinking by a recovering alcoholic; also called a slip. May be planned or unplanned.

Secular Organizations For Sobriety (SOS) A support group for alcoholics focusing on self-empowerment, self responsibility and human support. Believes that religion and sobriety are separate issues.

Sleep Apnea A disorder in which the upper air passage narrows or closes during sleep. Apnea wakens the person who then resumes breathing and returns to sleep. Apnea can occur hundreds of times each night, significantly reducing sleep time resulting in daytime sleepiness.

Sober A state where no alcohol or other mind altering substance has been used.

Sobriety An alcohol-free life.

Spirituality An inner peace, feeling of serenity, a process by which calm is restored after chaos. Does not mean the same as formalized religion.

Stigma of alcoholism Accepting the belief that alcoholism is a failure of self-will, and not a disease.

Tolerance A reduced response to alcohol over a period of exposure which results in a need to increase the amount of alcohol consumed in order to obtain the desired effect. Caused by the brain and liver adapting to increasing amounts of alcohol in the body.

Treatment Program in which the alcohol abuser or alcoholic and his or her family begin the process of recovery from alcohol abuse or alcoholism.

Wernicke-Korsakoff's Caused by alcohol's effect on the brain.
Syndrome Symptoms include short-term memory loss, disorientation and emotional disturbances.

Withdrawal Signs and symptoms experienced by the alcoholic when drinking stops or is drastically reduced.

Women For Sobriety A support group specifically for women
(WFS) alcoholics. Uses Thirteen Acceptance Statements.

Don't wait for your ship to come in; swim out to it.

Anonymous

SUGGESTED READING

There are many books about the various aspects of alcohol abuse and alcoholism. This listing is by no means complete but will get you started and help you find a book in an area that is of particular interest.

General Interest

Alcoholics Anonymous. New York: Alcoholics Anonymous World Service, 1993.

Baum, D. *Smoke and Mirrors: The War on Drugs and the Politics of Failure*. Boston: Little, Brown and Company, 1996.

Kinney, Jean and Gwen Leaton. *Loosening the Grip: A Handbook of Alcohol Information*. New York: McGraw Hill, 1994.

Kirkpatrick, Jean. *Goodbye Hangovers, Hello Life: Self Help for Women*. New York: Atheneum, 1986.

Milam, James R. and Katherine Ketcham. *Under The Influence: A Guide to the Myths and Realities of Alcoholism*. New York: Bantam, 1987.

Milhorn, H. Thomas. *Drug and Alcohol Abuse: The Alternative Guide for Parents, Teachers and Counselors*. New York: Plenum Press, 1994.

Trimpey, Jack. *Rational Recovery: The New Cure for Substance Addiction*. New York: Pocket Books, 1996.

Trimpey, Jack. *The Small Book: A Revolutionary Alternative for Overcoming Alcohol and Drug Dependence*. New York: Delacorte Press, 1992.

Twelve Steps and Twelve Traditions. New York: Alcoholics Anonymous World Service, 1994.

Vaillant, George E. *The Natural History of Alcoholism Revisited.* Cambridge: Harvard University Press, 1995.

Intervention

Johnson, Vernon E. *Intervention: How to Help Someone Who Doesn't want Help: A Step-by-Step Guide for Families of Chemically Dependent Persons.* Minneapolis: Johnson Institute Press, 1989.

Rogers, Ronald L. and Chandler Scott McMillin. *Freeing Someone You Love from Alcohol and Other Drugs.* Los Angeles: Price Stern Sloan, Inc., 1989.

Treatment

Beasley, Joseph D., MD. *Food for Recovery: The Complete Nutritional Companion for Recovering Alcoholics.* New York: Crown, 1994.

Beasley, Joseph D., MD. *How to Defeat Alcoholism: Nutritional Guidelines for Getting Sober.* New York: Times Books, 1989.

Christopher, James. *SOS Sobriety: The Proven Alternative to 12 Step Programs.* New York: Prometheus Books, 1992.

Geller, Anne, MD with M.J. Territo. *Restore Your Life: A Living Plan for Sober People.* New York: Bantam Books, 1991.

Ketcham, Katherine and L. Ann Mueller, MD. *Eating Right to Live Sober.* New York: Penguin Books, 1983.

Larson, Joan Mathews, Ph.D. *Seven Weeks to Sobriety: The Proven Program to Fight Alcoholism through Nutrition.* New York: Fawcett Books, 1997.

Mueller, L. Ann, MD and Katherine Ketcham. *Recovering: How to Get and Stay Sober.* New York: Bantam Books, 1987.

Personal Stories

Dorris, Michael. *The Broken Cord.* New York: Harper Perennial, 1990.

Fisher, Carrie. *Postcards from the Edge.* New York: Pocket Books, 1990.

Ford, Betty with Chris Chase. *A Glad Awakening.* New York: Doubleday, 1987.

Ford, Betty with Chris Chase. *The Times of My Life.* New York: Ballantine Books, 1979.

Hamill, Pete. *A Drinking Life.* Boston: Little, Brown and Company, 1995.

Knapp, Caroline. *Drinking: A Love Story.* New York: Delta Books, 1996.

McGovern, George. *Terry: My Daughters Life-and-Death Struggle with Alcoholism.* New York: Plume, 1997.

Robertson, Nan. *Getting Better: Inside Alcoholics Anonymous.* New York: William Morrow & Company, Inc., 1988.

Family Issues

Black, Claudia. *Double Duty: Dual Dynamic within the Chemically Dependent Home.* New York: Ballantine Books, 1990.

Drews, Toby Rice. *Getting Them Sober: You can Help*, Volume One. Baltimore: Recovery Communications, Inc., 1998.

Drews, Toby Rice. *Getting Them Sober: Volume Two*. South Plainfield, NJ: Bridge-Logos Publishers, 1984.

Rogers, Ronald L. and Chandler Scott McMillin. *If It Runs in Your Family: Alcoholism*. New York: Bantam Books, 1992.

Woititz, Janet Geringer, Ph.D. *Adult Children Of Alcoholics*. Deerfield Beach, Florida: Health Communications, 1990.

INDEX

Order Information

To acquire a copy of *Alcohol Abuse: Straight Talk, Straight Answers*:

- Call: Toll Free (800) 356-9315.
  American Express, Discover, Mastercard and Visa accepted.

- The book is available from your favorite online bookstore.

- The book is available from your local bookstore.

- E-mail: orders@UpperAccess.com

- Fax: Toll Free (800) 242-0036

- For quantity discounts contact:

Ixia Publications
Special Sales Department
350 Ward Avenue, Suite 106
Honolulu, HI 96814, USA